Table of Contents

Code: 1091

D1457985

. . . continued on next page

... continued from previous page

A Better Directory

Picking home improvement pros can be a nerve-wracking game of chance.

Who will be honest enough to say what's really needed? Who won't overcharge? Who will get the job done on time? Who'll clean up their messes?

Done Right!® takes the chance and worry out of home repairs and improvements. Our carefully pre-screened and relentlessly reviewed home pros will do the job right. *We guarantee it!*

Pre-Screened

- Our home pros have their licenses in order;
- They carry the proper amount and type of insurance; and
- They don't have unresolved complaints with the Houston BBB (Better Business Bureau) or the State of Houston, and if they do, they are taking appropriate, good faith steps to resolve them.

Relentlessly Reviewed

- Our home pros are enthusiastically endorsed by Realtors®, home inspectors, civil engineers, property managers and other picky, demanding trade professionals; and
- Our pros are only as good as their last job. We constantly gather customer feedback. Negatively reviewed pros—that don't move swiftly to make things right—are kicked out. Period.

Guaranteed

- Pros displaying the Done Right Guarantee®* logo are covered by the guarantee. If there's a problem, Done Right! steps in and facilitates a solution. Should the situation not be recoverable, Done Right! will pay for another pro to do the work right or reimburse the customer up to $1000.

  👍 Guaranteed

- If you have a bad experience with one of our pros, contact us at **1-800-494-6005 - Option 2** or via email at **Trouble@DoneRight.com.** Even if you haven't registered for the Done Right Guarantee, we will *always* help.

Free to Use

The Done Right Directory® is 100% FREE to use! Just call the pros of your choice using the given toll-free number. Feel free to use the Done Right Directory as much or as often as you'd like. That's what we're here for!

* Terms and conditions of the Done Right Guarantee are available at www.DoneRight.com. The Done Right Privacy Policy is available at www.doneright.com/PrivacyPolicy.cfm

Contacting Done Right!

Review a Done Right! Pro
Visit www.DoneRight.com
Click "Satisfaction Survey"

Report a Bad Experience
1-800-494-6005, Option 2
Trouble@DoneRight.com

Become a Done Right! Pro
1-800-936-0882
Sales@DoneRight.com

Mailing Address
Done Right!
35 E. Colorado Blvd.
Pasadena, CA 91105
Online: www.DoneRight.com

Note: Memberships (such as the BBB), associations and licenses
were valid at the time that this book was printed.

Map & Symbols

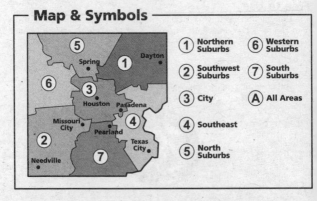

1 Northern Suburbs   6 Western Suburbs

2 Southwest Suburbs   7 South Suburbs

3 City   A All Areas

4 Southeast

5 North Suburbs

ADDITIONS

AMS REMODELING

👍 Guaranteed

③

Address: 2107 Lou Ellen Ln.
Houston, TX 77018

(800) 953-5449

In Business Since: 1988

Best At: All Home Remodeling, Bathroom Remodels, Complete Remodels, Custom Additions, Garages, Major Remodeling, New Homes, Room Additions

Associations & Certifications: Better Business Bureau, Texas Residential Construction Commission

Other Categories: Contractors - General Contractors

Testimonials:

I can't say enough about AMS Remodeling! I have used them personally and I have recommended their service to many of my clients.-Realtor

---

SAGE BUILT HOMES, LLC

👍 Guaranteed

③

Address: 2855 Mangum Rd., Suite 412
Houston, TX 77092

(888) 847-0943

In Business Since: 2005

Best At: Bathrooms, Complete Remodels, Consultation, Custom Additions, Design, Kitchens, Major Remodeling, New Homes

Associations & Certifications: Greater Houston Builders Association, Texas Residential Construction Commission

Testimonials:

Scott and his guys did a fantastic job building our new addition and remodeling our house. I highly recommend them to anyone looking to work with them. He's very detail-oriented and did a great job. We appreciated having him on board.-Consumer

We guarantee the services
of all pros displaying the
Done Right Guarantee® logo.

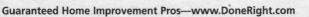

AIR CONDITIONING—REPAIR & MAINTENANCE

ARS/RESCUE ROOTER
(888) 875-7591

👍 Guaranteed

Ⓐ

In Business Since: 1979
License Number: TACLB00010268E
Best At: Central Air Cleaners, Central Air Conditioning, Central Humidifiers, Thermostats
Associations & Certifications: Plumbing-Heating-Cooling Contractors Association
Other Categories: Heating & Cooling - Repair & Maintenance, Plumbing - Drain & Sewer

---

ANDERSON HEATING & AIR, INC.
(877) 202-4163

👍 Guaranteed

①②③⑤⑥

In Business Since: 1992
License Number: TACLA00006747C
Best At: Air Conditioners, Air Distribution & Air Flow, Air Filtration, Central Air, Energy Efficiency, Forced Air Units, Maintenance & Tune-up, Retrofits, Routine Scheduled Maintenance, Upgrades
Other Categories: Heating & Cooling - Repair & Maintenance
Testimonials:

Anderson Heating & Air is very honest, tidy, and friendly. I have recommended their services to many people and have had no complaints whatsoever.-Consumer

---

JAY'S REFRIGERATION A/C & HEATING
(888) 787-0318

👍 Guaranteed

②③⑥

In Business Since: 1993
License Number: TACLB00013930E
Best At: All Brands & Models, Compressors, Emergency Service, Energy Efficiency, Forced Air Units, Humidifiers & Dehumidifiers, Maintenance & Tune-up, Replacement, Service, Thermostats
Brands: Trane®
Other Categories: Heating & Cooling - Repair & Maintenance
Testimonials:

I have done business with Jay's Refrigeration for some time now. He is very reliable, and does terrific work. I recommend him every chance I get.-Consumer

AIR CONDITIONING—REPAIR & MAINTENANCE CONT'D

SUNBELT AIR CONDITIONING & HEATING

 Guaranteed

③

Address: 7407 Shady Vale Ln.
Houston, TX 77040

(866) 758-5220

In Business Since: 1992
License Number: TACLB00010628E
Best At: Air Conditioners, Air Distribution & Air Flow, Air Ducts, Air Filtration, Compressors, Emergency Service, Forced Air Units, Replacement, Upgrades
Brands: Carrier®, Frigidaire®, Goodman®
Special Offers: 6 Month Warranty On Repairs, One Year Warranty on Installation
Associations & Certifications: Better Business Bureau
Other Categories: Heating & Cooling - Repair & Maintenance
Testimonials:

> We have been using Sunbelt for over 14 years. They always do great work and have yet to be under-bid for any job we have had for them. We have and will continue to recommend them to anyone needing their services..-Realtor

POPULAR HVAC SERVICES

Guaranteed

③

Address: 7426 Yellow Pine Dr.
Houston, TX 77040

(888) 233-8583

In Business Since: 2004
License Number: TACLB00023855E
Best At: Air Filtration, Central Air Cleaners, Central Air Conditioning, Compressors, Energy Efficiency, Routine Scheduled Maintenance, Thermostats, Ducts, Forced Air Units, Humidifiers & Dehumidifiers
Special Offers: 12 Months No Payments/No Interest
Associations & Certifications: Better Business Bureau
Testimonials:

> Popular HVAC has performed both residential and commercial work for the past 2 years. They do a great job! Many of us have used his services on a personal level.-Realtor

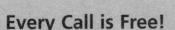

Every Call is Free!

AIR CONDITIONING—SALES & INSTALLATION

ARS/RESCUE ROOTER
(888) 875-7626

In Business Since: 1979
License Number: TACLB00010268E
Best At: Central Air Cleaners, Central Air Conditioning, Central Humidifiers, Thermostat Replace or Reprogram
Associations & Certifications: Plumbing-Heating-Cooling Contractors Association
Other Categories: Electricians, Emergency - Electricians, Emergency - Plumbing, Heating & Cooling - Sales & Installation, Plumbing - Contractors

---

SEARS HOME
IMPROVEMENT PRODUCTS
(888) 277-9935

In Business Since: 1984
License Number: TACLB00019160E
Best At: Air Conditioners, Central Air, Energy Efficiency
Brands: Carrier®, Kenmore®
Special Offers: Free Estimates
Associations & Certifications: Better Business Bureau, ENERGY STAR
Other Categories: Heating & Cooling - Sales & Installation

ANDERSON HEATING
& AIR, INC.
(877) 203-7238

In Business Since: 1992
License Number: TACLA00006747C
Best At: Air Conditioners, Air Distribution & Air Flow, Central Air, Custom Indoor Comfort System, Designing HVAC Systems, Energy Efficiency, Forced Air Units, Installation, Retrofits, Upgrades
Other Categories: Heating & Cooling - Sales & Installation
Testimonials:

Anderson Heating & Air is very honest, tidy, and friendly. I have recommended their services to many people and had no complaints whatsoever.-Consumer

Every Call is Free!

AIR CONDITIONING—SALES & INSTALLATION CONT'D

JAY'S REFRIGERATION A/C & HEATING
(888) 826-1731

In Business Since: 1993
License Number: TACLB00013930E
Best At: Air Balancing, Air Cleaners, Air Conditioners, Air Distribution & Air Flow, Air Ducts, Air Filtration, Air Purification, Air Quality Testing, Central Air
Brands: Trane®
Other Categories: Heating & Cooling - Sales & Installation
Testimonials:

I have done business with Jay's Refrigeration for some time now. He is very reliable and does terrific work. I recommend him every chance I get.-Consumer

AIR QUALITY—AIR PURIFICATION SYSTEMS

See Heating & Cooling—Sales & Installation. 64

AIR QUALITY—DUCT CLEANING

SEARS CARPET, UPHOLSTERY & AIR DUCT CLEANING
(877) 416-3816

In Business Since: 1995
Best At: Remove Allergens, Remove Dirt, Debris & Dust
Special Offers: Discount for Done Right! Customers
Associations & Certifications: Better Business Bureau, Carpet & Rug Institute's Gold Seal of Approval
Other Categories: Carpet - Cleaning, Emergency - Carpet Cleaning, Grout Cleaning, Tile & Stone - Cleaning, Upholstery - Cleaning & Restoration

MBM CLEANING
Address: 6423 Atwell Dr.
Houston, TX 77081
(888) 249-8427

In Business Since: 2000
Best At: Air Ducts, Air Filtration, Indoor Air Quality, Remove Allergens, Remove Dirt, Debris & Dust
Associations & Certifications: Better Business Bureau, Institute of Inspection, Cleaning & Restoration Certification, National Air Duct Cleaners Association (NADCA)
Testimonials:

MBM Cleaning does a tremendously clean job. -Consumer

ARBORIST

TEXAS TREE TEAM
(800) 949-5887

Ⓐ

In Business Since: 1997
Best At: Brush Chipping, Brush Trimming, Crown Reduction, Fire Prevention & Clean-up, Hedges, Insect & Disease Control, Irrigation, Pruning, Removal, Repair, Structural Trimming, Thinning, Tree & Shrub Planting, Tree & Stump Removal, Tree Trimming
Special Offers: Free Estimates
Associations & Certifications: Professional Landcare Network (PLANET)

OLVERA TREE SERVICES, INC.
(800) 934-6771

①③⑤

In Business Since: 1994
Best At: Brush Trimming, Pruning, Removal, Stump Removal, Thinning, Tree & Stump Removal, Tree Trimming
Special Offers: Free Estimates
Associations & Certifications: Better Business Bureau
Testimonials:

Olvera Tree Services has cut down several trees as well as done tree maintenance for me. They always work hard and do a good job. I will continue to use their service.-Consumer

---

FALL LANDSCAPE

Address: 16318 Alametos Dr.
Houston, TX 77083

(800) 934-3554

Ⓖⓤⓐⓡⓐⓝⓣⓔⓔⓓ

②③⑥

In Business Since: 1992
Best At: Brush Chipping, Brush Trimming, Hedges, Pruning, Removal, Tree & Shrub Planting, Tree & Stump Removal, Tree Trimming
Special Offers: Free Estimates
Testimonials:

We've worked with him for quite a while now. He's always done a great job for us. We love working with him. He's responsive, on time, does a good job, and we highly recommend him.-General Contractor

Every Call is Free!

BATHROOM—FIXTURE REPAIR & REFINISH

BATHROOM FIXTURES

ARS/RESCUE ROOTER (888) 219-8195

Ⓐ

In Business Since: 1979
License Number: M-17251
Best At: Faucets, Garbage Disposals, Installation, Piping, Repair, Showers, Sinks, Toilets, Tubs
Brands: American Standard, Delta®, GROHE, Kohler®, Moen®, TOTO®
Associations & Certifications: Plumbing-Heating-Cooling Contractors Association

BATHROOM REMODELING

FLOOR COVERINGS & MORE, INC.

Ⓐ

Address: 2395 Highway 6 South, Suite F
Houston, TX 77077

(877) 464-7037

In Business Since: 1989
Best At: Additions, Bathroom Fixtures & Accessories, Cabinet Refacing, Cabinets, Complete Remodels, Counter Tops, Custom Work, Flooring, Tile
Brands: KraftMaid
Special Offers: Two Year Financing with No Interest
Associations & Certifications: Texas Residential Construction Commission
Other Categories: Remodeling - Kitchens
Testimonials:
I highly recommend Floor Coverings & More. They are very friendly and easy to deal with.-Consumer

We guarantee the services
of all pros displaying the
Done Right Guarantee® logo.

BATHROOM REMODELING CONT'D

LARR-WOOD CONSTRUCTION

👍 **Guaranteed**

①②③⑤⑥

Address: 19515 Wied Rd., Suite B
Spring, TX 77388

(877) 465-7795

In Business Since: 2001
Best At: Complete Remodels, Counter Tops, Cabinets, Repair, Restoration, Additions, Flooring, Sinks
Special Offers: Satisfaction Guarantee
Associations & Certifications: Texas Residential Construction Commission
Other Categories: Remodeling - Kitchens
Testimonials:

> I've used Larr-Wood for over 6 years now. All I can say is that Larry has the most professional and reliable company. His crew does excellent work, and I have recommended Larr-Wood to everyone who needed his services.-General Contractor

We guarantee the services

of all pros displaying the

Done Right Guarantee® logo.

Map & Symbols

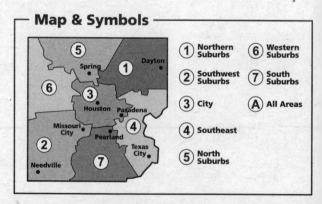

① **Northern Suburbs**	⑥ **Western Suburbs**
② **Southwest Suburbs**	⑦ **South Suburbs**
③ **City**	Ⓐ **All Areas**
④ **Southeast**	
⑤ **North Suburbs**	

BATHTUBS & SINKS—REPAIR & REFINISH

911 PLUMBING
(888) 843-4251

In Business Since: 1990
License Number: M-37412
Best At: Bathtubs, Hydro Cleaning, Parts, Sinks, Wash Basins
Special Offers: Discount for Done Right! Customers, Senior Citizen Discount
Testimonials:

We use 911 Plumbing on all of our store locations plumbing needs. They show up and do the job that needs to be done.-Multi-unit Rental Property Owner/ Manager

TUBS & TOPS
(888) 610-1009

👍 Guaranteed
Ⓐ

In Business Since: 1986
Best At: Bathtubs, Fixture Resurfacing, Porcelain, Porcelain Chip Repair, Sinks, Wash Basins
Testimonials:

Tubs and Tops has done a few jobs for us. They have repaired and resurfaced tubs for us, as well as resurfaced some counter tops. I would definitely recommend their services to others.-Consumer

BLINDS

PRICED RIGHT BLINDS AND SHUTTERS

👍 Guaranteed
Ⓐ

Address: 17607 Lonesome Dove Trails
Houston, TX 77095

(888) 268-9443

In Business Since: 1957
Best At: Faux Blinds, In-home Consultation, Design Preview, Motorized Blinds, Shutters, Wood Blinds
Other Categories: Shutters
Testimonials:

Priced Right Blinds and Shutters does great work and has excellent prices. I highly recommend his services.-Consumer

Every Call is Free!

Home Improvement Pros and Home Services

Free to Use and Guaranteed*

BLINDS CONT'D

HOUSTON DESIGN CENTER
👍 Guaranteed

Address: 115951 FM 529, #115
Houston, TX 77095

(888) 212-8664
In Business Since: 2003
Best At: Custom Made Draperies, Swags, Cascades, & Cornices, Custom Window Coverings, Shades, Shutters, Valances, Window Coverings, Mini Blinds
Brands: Hunter Douglas, Skandia, Timber Blind & Shutter
Special Offers: Free Estimates, Free Installation
Testimonials:
Houston Design Center was very professional, knowledgeable and precise. I was extremely impressed with their work.-Consumer

JINGA HOUSE OF WINDOW FASHIONS
👍 Guaranteed

①③⑤

(888) 868-6797
In Business Since: 2007
Best At: 100s of Design Ideas, Cellular, Custom Made Draperies, Swags, Cascades, & Cornices, In-home Consultation, Installation, Arched & Angled Windows, Blinds, Shutters
Brands: ADO, Graber®, Hunter Douglas, Kensington
Testimonials:
We were very happy with the work performed by Jinga House. We are planning on using their service again in the near future.-Consumer

We guarantee the services of all pros displaying the **Done Right Guarantee® logo**.

CABINETS

MILLTEX CONSTRUCTION CO., INC.

Address: 6911 Breen
Houston, TX 77086

(888) 567-9557

In Business Since: 1990

Best At: Counter Tops, Custom Cabinets, Custom Design, Custom Laminate, Custom Wood Work, Design Center, Kitchens, New Cabinets, New Custom Door & Drawer Fronts, Pre-finished Cabinetry

Testimonials:

Milltex Construction Co. is very helpful in planning, and up front with every-thing.-Consumer

CABINETS REFACING

SEARS HOME IMPROVEMENT PRODUCTS

(877) 332-6796

In Business Since: 1984

Best At: 100s of Drawer & Cabinet Styles & Colors, Custom Cabinet Refacing, Hardware, Matching Handles, Turnkey Installation

Brands: Aristokraft®, Zodiaq®

Special Offers: Free Estimates

Associations & Certifications: Better Business Bureau, ENERGY STAR

CARPENTERS

HANDYMAN CONNECTION

Address: 5320 Gulfton St., Suite 14
Houston, TX 77081

(877) 227-3541

In Business Since: 1993

Best At: Carpentry, Crown Molding, Decks, Doors, Dry Rot Repair, Finish Carpentry, Interior & Exterior Restoration, Interior Doors & Trim, Repair

Special Offers: Free Estimates

Associations & Certifications: Better Business Bureau

Other Categories: Handyman

Every Call is Free!

CARPENTERS CONT'D

GOSEN GENERAL CONTRACTORS, INC.

Address: 10101 Southwest Freeway, Suite 315-320
Houston, TX 77074

(888) 225-3449

In Business Since: 1992
Best At: Built-ins, Cabinets, Custom Cabinets, Custom Work, Decks, Framing, Gazebos, Interior & Exterior Restoration, Interior Moldings, Kitchen & Bathroom Cabinets, Mantels, Wood Paneling
Associations & Certifications: Better Business Bureau
Other Categories: Handyman

BAY AREA PAINT & TILE
(888) 212-2621

In Business Since: 1985
Best At: Baseboards, Cabinets, Closets, Crown Molding, Custom Trim, Decks, Decorative Trim, Doors, Finish Trim, Framework, Interior Doors & Trim
Special Offers: New Customer Discount
Associations & Certifications: Better Business Bureau
Other Categories: Handyman

CARPET & VINYL—SALES & INSTALLATION

GOLDEN GREEK CARPETS, INC.

Address: 4525 S. Pinemont Dr., #170
Houston, TX 77041

(888) 397-6227

In Business Since: 1975
Best At: Carpet, Full Service Flooring, In-home Consultation, Laminates, Next Day Installation, Shop-At-Home Service, Vinyl
Associations & Certifications: American Flooring Alliance, Building Owners and Managers Association, Houston Apartment Association, World Floor Covering Association
Testimonials:
They've done a few jobs for me. My customers have been very, very happy with them. They know what they are doing, they get the job done, and they clean up after themselves. They are a good company. When customers ask for carpet, I always refer out to Golden Greek.-General Contractor

CARPET & VINYL—SALES & INSTALLATION CONT'D

WAYNE'S CARPET & OAK FLOORING

Address: 11633 Katy Fwy.
Houston, TX 77079

(888) 490-9220

In Business Since: 1982
Best At: Area Rugs, Berber, Custom Carpets, Design Center, Installation, Kitchens, Laminates
Associations & Certifications: Better Business Bureau
Testimonials:

> Wayne's Carpet & Oak Flooring did an excellent job installing wood flooring in my house. I would definitely use their service again and I have highly recommended their services to others.-Consumer

---

PATTERSON CARPETS & INTERIORS, INC.

Address: 7026 Old Katy Rd., Suite 292
Houston, TX 77024

(888) 210-3417

In Business Since: 1991
Best At: Berber, Custom Carpets, Design Center, Installation
Associations & Certifications: Better Business Bureau
Testimonials:

> They do a great job. They follow through to the completion with every project I have them do.-Consumer

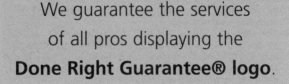

We guarantee the services
of all pros displaying the
Done Right Guarantee® logo.

2008—Fall—Houston Metro Directory

CARPET—CLEANING

SEARS CARPET, UPHOLSTERY & AIR DUCT CLEANING
(888) 294-5786

In Business Since: 1995
Best At: Carpet & Upholstery Cleaning, Carpet & Rug Protection, Deep Cleaning, Deodorizing, Oriental Rugs, Stain Removal, Two-step Deep-clean Process, Carpet Repairs
Special Offers: Discount for Done Right! Customers
Associations & Certifications: Better Business Bureau, Carpet & Rug Institute's Gold Seal of Approval
Other Categories: Duct Cleaning, Emergency - Carpet Cleaning, Grout Cleaning, Tile & Stone - Cleaning, Upholstery - Cleaning & Restoration

OOPS STEAM CLEANING
(888) 563-5952

In Business Since: 2006
Best At: All Carpet Damage, Area Rugs, Bleach Spot Removal, Damage Restoration, Deep Steam Cleaning, Oriental Rugs, Rugs, Stain Removal, Upholstery Cleaning, Water Damage, Water Extraction
Other Categories: Upholstery - Cleaning & Restoration

ABSOLUTE KLEEN
(888) 829-4809

In Business Since: 1981
Best At: Area Rugs, Carpet Repairs, Commercial, Deodorizing, Emergency Service, Oriental Rugs, Pet Odor Removal, Re-stretching, Stain Removal, Upholstery Cleaning
Special Offers: One Year Warranty
Associations & Certifications: Better Business Bureau
Other Categories: Emergency - Carpet Cleaning
Testimonials:
They did a great job in re-stretching my carpet. They are very experienced in what they do. I highly recommend them.-Consumer

Every Call is Free!

CARPET—CLEANING CONT'D

BLUE RIBBON CARPET CARE   🖒 Guaranteed

Address: P.O. Box 720055
Houston, TX 77099   ②③⑥

(888) 595-9889

In Business Since: 1991
Best At: Carpet & Upholstery Cleaning, Carpet Repairs, Deodorizing, Fast Drying, Pet Odor Removal, Stain Removal
Special Offers: 100% Satisfaction Guarantee, Free Preconditioning with Service
Associations & Certifications: Institute of Inspection, Cleaning & Restoration Certification
Testimonials:

> Blue Ribbon Carpet Care went above and beyond what I expected from them. I am very happy with their service and the job they did. I would definitely use them again and I have recommended them to others needing carpet cleaning.- Consumer

CARPET—REPAIR

SEARS CARPET, UPHOLSTERY & AIR DUCT CLEANING   🖒 Guaranteed
(877) 569-4298   Ⓐ

In Business Since: 1995
Best At: Buckle Repairs, Pad Replacements, Pet Damage, Re-tuck, Patching, Rip Repairs, Deodorizing, Stretching
Special Offers: Discount for Done Right! Customers
Associations & Certifications: Better Business Bureau, Carpet & Rug Institute's Gold Seal of Approval

─ Map & Symbols ─

① Northern Suburbs	⑥ Western Suburbs
② Southwest Suburbs	⑦ South Suburbs
③ City	Ⓐ All Areas
④ Southeast	
⑤ North Suburbs	

CLEANING—MAIDS & CLEANING SERVICES

MERRY MAIDS
(888) 798-4678

(A)

In Business Since: 1979
Best At: Complete Home Cleaning, Housekeeping, Maid Service, Move-ins & Move-outs, Special Occasion Cleaning, Spring/Fall House Cleaning
Other Categories: Emergency - Maids

MAID BRIGADE
(800) 889-5190

Guaranteed
Green Merchant
①③④⑤⑦

In Business Since: 1979
Best At: Bathrooms, Bi-weekly, Common Area, Complete Home Cleaning, Kitchens, Monthly, Move-ins & Move-outs, Weekly
Associations & Certifications: Green Clean Certification

HOLY MAID
(877) 257-2909

Guaranteed
③

In Business Since: 2005
Best At: All Living Areas, Bathrooms, Bedrooms, Carpet Cleaning, Floors, Kitchens, Mirrors, Remove Clutter, Trash, Vacuuming
Testimonials:
> Holy Maid has been cleaning for a while now. They are prompt, never miss an appointment and do a very nice job.-General Contractor

CLEANING—WATER & FIRE DAMAGE

See Water & Fire Damage—Repair & Restoration 103

CLOSETS

MCCAIN KITCHEN & BATH

Address: 9815 Hughes Ranch Rd.
Houston, TX 77089

(800) 934-1669

In Business Since: 1981
Best At: All Closet Types, Cabinets, Entertainment Centers, Installation, Roll-out Shelving
Testimonials:

McCain Kitchen & Bath did a great job on our home. They were timely and cleaned up after themselves. I will use them again.-Consumer

COMPUTER—REPAIRS AND NETWORKING

REBOOT REMEDY

Address: 8310 Castleford St., Suite 230
Houston, TX 77040

(877) 444-8662

In Business Since: 1994
Best At: Networking, Service, Web Design
Brands: Acer, Dell™, Gateway®, HP, Toshiba
Testimonials:

Everything was great. They did good work. They designed a website for me and it was really nice.-Consumer

TYBER PC

Address: 6133 FM 1960 West
Houston, TX 77069

(888) 269-3119

In Business Since: 1996
Best At: Data Recovery, Memory & Hard Drive Upgrades, Spyware Removal, Virus Protection, Virus Removal, All Brands & Models
Brands: Intel®, Microsoft®
Testimonials:

Tyber PC did an excellent job on fixing my computer. I have and will continue to recommend them to all of my friends.-Consumer

CONCRETE

CONCRETE—CONTRACTORS

TEXAS LONE STAR PAVEMENT SERVICES, INC.

Guaranteed ①②③⑤⑥

Address: 27045 Hanna Rd.
Conroe, TX 77385

(888) 234-3114

In Business Since: 1994
Best At: Cement, Colored Concrete, Concrete Removal, Curbs, Driveways, Flat Work, Grading, Parking Lots, Residential & Commercial, Sealing, Sidewalks, Staining, Faux Brick
Brands: Artcrete®
Special Offers: Free Estimates
Testimonials:
> We've used Texas Lone Star Pavement Services for 3-4 years now. They do very good work and I highly recommend their services.-Multi-unit Rental Property Owner/Manager

IMPRESSIONS IN CONCRETE

Guaranteed ①②③⑤⑥

Address: 6213 Peg St.
Houston, TX 77092

(888) 242-9319

In Business Since: 1992
Best At: Acid Staining, Colored Concrete, Decorative, Driveways, Flat Work, Overlays, Parking Lots, Patios, Pool Decks, Residential & Commercial, Stamped Concrete, Textured Concrete
Special Offers: Free Estimates
Associations & Certifications: Better Business Bureau
Testimonials:
> Their company is excellent. I build restaurants, and they've done quite a bit of stamped concrete for me. They're one of the best contractors that I deal with.-General Contractor

ARTISAN CONCRETE DESIGN, LLC

Guaranteed ①②③⑤⑥

(800) 830-5997

In Business Since: 2004
Best At: Acid Staining, Colored Concrete, Concrete Removal, Concrete Resurfacing, Driveways, Flat Work, Non-slip Sealer, Overlays, Patios, Pool Decks, Residential & Commercial, Resurfacing, Stamped Concrete
Special Offers: Free Estimates
Testimonials:
> He did work for me on a couple of different projects. The work was fine. They did a nice job. I absolutely recommend them.-General Contractor

1111111111111111111111111111111111111111111111111111111111111111111111111111111111111

CONTRACTORS—ELECTRICAL

For major electrical work, a licensed electrician is an absolute must.

ARS/RESCUE ROOTER
(866) 269-8883

Guaranteed

Ⓐ

In Business Since: 1979
License Number: 18810
Best At: Attic or Whole House Fans, Ceiling Fans, Exhaust Fans, Fixtures, Installation, Lighting, Outlets, Panel Upgrades, Switches, Thermostat Replacement, Wiring
Associations & Certifications: Plumbing-Heating-Cooling Contractors Association
Other Categories: Air Conditioning - Sales & Installation, Emergency - Electricians, Emergency - Plumbing, Heating & Cooling - Sales & Installation, Plumbing - Contractors

UNIVERSAL WIRING

Guaranteed

Ⓐ

Address: P.O. Box 30467
Houston, TX 77249

(888) 843-4228

In Business Since: 1992
License Number: 17525
Best At: Circuit Breakers & Fuses, Dedicated Circuits, Electrical Service Upgrades, Emergency Service, Home Re-wiring, Interior Wiring, Lighting Design & Installation, Meter & Panel Rewires, New Home Trouble Shooting, Outlets, Panel Upgrades, Switches, Troubleshooting
Brands: Cutler-Hammer®, HALO®, Leviton®, Lightolier®, Square D®
Special Offers: Discount for Done Right! Customers, Three Year Warranty on All Repairs
Associations & Certifications: Better Business Bureau
Other Categories: Emergency - Electricians
Testimonials:
Ed did a great job and I would recommend him to other clients-Consumer

KENMOR ELECTRIC CO., LP

Guaranteed

Ⓐ

Address: 8330 Hansen Rd.
Houston, TX 77075

(888) 805-8390

In Business Since: 1976
License Number: 29130
Best At: Amp Service & Amp Upgrades, Ceiling Fans, Circuit Breakers & Fuses, Construction, Dedicated Circuits, Electrical Service Upgrades, Remodeling, Repair, Switches, Lighting
Brands: Home Craftsman
Special Offers: 100% Satisfaction Guarantee, One Year Warranty
Associations & Certifications: American Subcontractors Association - Houston Chapter (ASA)
Other Categories: Emergency - Electricians
Testimonials:

CONTRACTORS—ELECTRICAL CONT'D

LOGO ELECTRICAL SERVICES, INC.

Address: 9506 Tallow Tree Dr.
Houston, TX 77070

(888) 841-1272

In Business Since: 2005
License Number: 23582
Best At: Aluminum Wiring, Ceiling Fans, Circuit Breakers & Fuses, Emergency Service, Home Re-wiring, Light Commercial, Lighting Design & Installation, Recessed Lighting, Service Upgrades, Troubleshooting
Special Offers: Discount for Done Right! Customers
Other Categories: Emergency - Electricians
Testimonials:

Logo Electrical Services is very reliable and professional. I highly recommend them.-General Contractor

---

G & A ELECTRIC CO.
(800) 970-2798

In Business Since: 1968
License Number: 11448
Best At: Additions, Bathrooms, Breakers, Computer & Phone Data Wiring, Electrical Service Upgrades, Emergency Service, Home Re-wiring, Light Commercial, Panel Upgrades, Residential Remodels
Testimonials:

G & A Electric Company has done great work for me. They are easy to work with, flexible with my schedule, prompt and reasonably priced.-Consumer

---

INCREDIBLE ELECTRIC

Address: P.O. Box 171
Spring, TX 77383

(888) 329-4094

In Business Since: 2003
License Number: 24677
Best At: Troubleshooting, Surge Protectors, Security Lighting, Recessed Lighting, Panel Upgrades, Outlets, Lighting Design & Installation, Emergency Service, Circuit Breakers & Fuses
Special Offers: Discount for Done Right! Customers, Free Inspection
Associations & Certifications: Better Business Bureau, Technician Seal of Safety™
Other Categories: Emergency - Electricians
Testimonials:

I've been using Albert as a subcontractor for over 6 years. He is incredibly knowledgeable and I completely trust his opinion. He does excellent work and amazes me with every job he completes. I always recommend him to anyone needing commercial or residential electrical work. -Consumer

Home Improvement Pros and Home Services

Free to Use and Guaranteed*

*Terms and conditions of the Done Right Guarantee® are at www.DoneRight.co

CONTRACTORS—GENERAL CONTRACTORS

For small home repairs, see our 'Handyman' category. For contractors that specialize in additions, bathrooms or kitchens, see our 'Remodeling' section.

K & S RENOVATIONS
(888) 214-5715

 Guaranteed

(A)

In Business Since: 1995
Best At: Additions, Bathroom Remodels, Kitchen Remodels, Complete Remodels
Special Offers: Senior Citizen Discount
Associations & Certifications: Better Business Bureau, Texas Residential Construction Commission
Testimonials:

K & S Renovations has done a complete renovation for me. I found them to be very reliable and they have proven to do great work. I will use them again when I have another remodeling project.-Consumer

---

AMS REMODELING
Address: 2107 Lou Ellen Ln.
Houston, TX 77018

(866) 262-5996

Guaranteed

(3)

In Business Since: 1988
Best At: Additions, Bathroom Remodels, Complete Remodels, Custom Homes, Full Service General Contractor, Garage Conversions, Major Renovations, New Construction, Remodeling
Associations & Certifications: Better Business Bureau, Texas Residential Construction Commission
Other Categories: Remodeling - New Additions
Testimonials:

I can't say enough about AMS Remodeling! I have used them personally and I have recommended their service to many of my clients.-Realtor

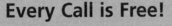

CONTRACTORS—PAINTING

BRUSHSTROKES PAINTING, INC.   👍 Guaranteed

Address: 17424 W. Grand Pkwy., #254
Sugar Land, TX 77479

Ⓐ

(888) 835-6784

BBB

In Business Since: 2000
Best At: Accent Colors, Brush, Color Consultation, Color Matching,
Complete Home Painting Interior and/or Exterior, Consultation with
Experienced Estimator, Custom Colors, Faux Finishing, Oil Base
Woodwork, Premium Quality Paint, Repainting, Whole House Painting
Associations & Certifications: Better Business Bureau
Testimonials:

*We've used them as a subcontractor for the Home Depot Paint Department for
the past two-and-a-half years. On a scale from 1 to 10, 10 being the highest,
they would get 10's in customer service and quality of work. We've never even
had a minor complaint about them.-General Contractor*

BAY AREA PAINT & TILE   👍 Guaranteed
(877) 451-5264   ①③④⑦

In Business Since: 1985
Best At: Brush, Color Consultation, Color Matching, Complete Home Painting
Interior and/or Exterior, Custom Colors, Custom Interior, Staining, Textures
Special Offers: New Customer Discount
Other Categories: Tile & Stone - Sales & Installation

Every Call is Free!

─ Map & Symbols ─

①	Northern Suburbs	⑥	Western Suburbs
②	Southwest Suburbs	⑦	South Suburbs
③	City	Ⓐ	All Areas
④	Southeast		
⑤	North Suburbs		

CONTRACTORS—PAINTING CONT'D

CERTAPRO PAINTERS
(800) 889-6536

 Guaranteed

In Business Since: 1992
Best At: Complimentary Color Consultation, Consultation with Experienced Estimator, Final Clean-up & Inspection, Furniture Protection, Premium Quality Paint, Site Preparation
Brands: Sherwin-Williams™
Associations & Certifications: Better Business Bureau, Chamber of Commerce
Other Categories: Painting - Exterior

BBB ACCREDITED BUSINESS

K & S RENOVATIONS
(888) 214-4938

Guaranteed

Ⓐ

In Business Since: 1995
Best At: Brush, Clean Drop Cloths, Color Consultation, Complete Home Painting Interior and/or Exterior
Associations & Certifications: Better Business Bureau, Texas Residential Construction Commission
Other Categories: Decks
Testimonials:

K & S Renovations has done a complete renovation for me. I found them to be very reliable and they have proven to do great work. I will use them again when I have another remodeling project.-Consumer

BBB ACCREDITED BUSINESS

MCCAIN KITCHEN & BATH

Guaranteed

Ⓐ

Address: 9815 Hughes Ranch Rd.
Houston, TX 77089

(800) 934-1339

In Business Since: 1981
Best At: Brush, Color Matching, Consultation, Cracks, Final Clean-up & Inspection, Premium Coating
Testimonials:

I was very pleased with the work McCain Kitchen & Bath did for me. I highly recommend them.-Consumer

We guarantee the services
of all pros displaying the
Done Right Guarantee® logo.

CONTRACTORS—PAINTING CONT'D

GOSEN GENERAL CONTRACTORS, INC.

Address: 10101 Southwest Freeway, Suite 315-320
Houston, TX 77074

(888) 878-8056

In Business Since: 1992
Best At: Cabinets, Carpentry, Caulking, Ceilings, Color Matching, Custom Work, Doors, Faux Finishing, Repainting, Staining, Textures, Whole House Painting
Brands: Benjamin Moore®, ICI Paints, Pittsburgh®, Sherwin-Williams™
Associations & Certifications: Better Business Bureau
Other Categories: Tile & Stone - Sales & Installation
Testimonials:

We've used Gosen General on several occasions, and we are always happy with their quality of work.-General Contractor

---

TURNKEY PAINTING, INC.

Address: 10422 Rockley Rd.
Houston, TX 77099

(888) 242-9307

In Business Since: 1992
Best At: Brush, Color Matching, Complete Home Painting Interior and/or Exterior, Crown Moldings, Faux Finishing, Interior & Exterior, Premium Quality Paint, Residential & Commercial, Textures, Trim, Walls, Whole House Painting, Wood Trim
Brands: PPG/Monarch Paint, Sherwin-Williams™
Associations & Certifications: Better Business Bureau
Testimonials:

Turnkey Painting proved to be dependable and I liked that they kept me updated on their progress. I would use their services again.-Consumer

We guarantee the services
of all pros displaying the
Done Right Guarantee® logo.

CONTRACTORS—PLUMBING

For major plumbing work, a licensed Plumbing
Contractor is an absolute must.

ARS/RESCUE ROOTER
(888) 422-1794

👍 Guaranteed

Ⓐ

In Business Since: 1979
License Number: M-17251
Best At: Complete Plumbing Needs, Faucets, Fixtures, Gas Lines, Interior
Foundation Drains, Leak Detection, Piping, Sewer Lines & Sewer Systems,
Sewer Main Clearing, Sump Pumps
Brands: American Standard, Delta®, GROHE, Kohler®, Moen®, TOTO®
Associations & Certifications: Plumbing-Heating-Cooling Contractors
Association
Other Categories: Air Conditioning - Sales & Installation, Electricians,
Emergency - Electricians, Emergency - Plumbing, Heating & Cooling - Sales &
Installation

SOUTHERN PLUMBING
SERVICES, LLC

👍 Guaranteed

Ⓐ

Address: 11806 Ainsworth Dr.
Stafford, TX 77477

(877) 315-3914

In Business Since: 2004
License Number: M - 36796
Best At: Cable Line Cleaning, Camera Inspection, Complete Plumbing Needs,
Emergency Service, Epoxy Pipe Lining, Fixtures, Gas Lines, Piping, Re-route,
Repair, Sewer Cleaning, Sewer Damage, Tankless Water Heaters, Water
Heaters, Water Lines & Pipes
Testimonials:

*Southern Plumbing Services has been providing service to us for the last 4-5
years. We continue to be happy with their service and the quality of their
work.-General Contractor*

Every Call is Free!

CONTRACTORS—PLUMBING CONT'D

ABERLE PLUMBING SERVICE (877) 400-7998

👍 Guaranteed

③

In Business Since: 1989
License Number: M-22759
Best At: Bathtubs, Camera Inspection, Complete Remodels, Drain Cleaning, Gas Lines, Hydro Jetting, Leak Detection, Sewer Cleaning, Showers, Tankless Water Heaters, Water Heaters, Water Purifiers & Water Softeners
Associations & Certifications: Better Business Bureau
Other Categories: Emergency - Plumbing
Testimonials:

> We've used Aberle Plumbing for about 6-7 years now. They do very good work and I highly recommend them.-General Contractor

JMT PLUMBING

👍 Guaranteed

③

Address: P.O. Box 1771
Baytown, TX 77522

(888) 739-1817

In Business Since: 2007
License Number: M-37917
Best At: Backflows, Bathtubs, Complete Plumbing Needs, Copper Re-piping, Drain Cleaning, Emergency Service, Faucets, Fixtures, Garbage Disposals, Gas Lines, Gas Re-piping, Inspecting & Testing, Leak Repairs, Plumbing, Plumbing Rearrangements, Polybutylene Plumbing Services, Repair, Service & Maintenance, Water Heaters, Sewer Cleaning, Showers, Sinks, Toilets, Water Drains
Special Offers: Military Discount, Senior Citizen Discount
Other Categories: Emergency - Plumbing
Testimonials:

> JMT Plumbing does fantastic work. I have used them on several occasions and they are always quick, clean and get the problem solved right. I highly recommend them.-Consumer

We guarantee the services
of all pros displaying the
Done Right Guarantee® logo.

CONTRACTORS—POOLS

CREATIVE LIFESTYLE POOLS (888) 841-1132

In Business Since: 1973
Best At: Concrete, Custom Pools, Custom Waterfalls
Testimonials:
> I have done business with Creative Lifestyle Pools for about 5 years. Jim is a great person to work with, and he always does a superb job. -General Contractor

CONTRACTORS—ROOFING

MURRAY ROOFING & CONSTRUCTION, LLC (877) 416-4844

In Business Since: 1977
Best At: Asphalt Shingles, Cedar Shake Roofs, Certifications, Clay Tile, Coating, Sealing & Finishing, Composition Shingles, Concrete Tile, Flat Roofs, Replacement Roofs
Testimonials:
> Murray Roofing was prompt, efficient, worked fast, cleaned up nicely, and kept us informed at all times. They did an overall great job.-Consumer

COUNTER TOPS

QUEEN OF THE TILE, INC. (866) 290-3885

In Business Since: 1999
Best At: Custom Countertops, Custom Design, Custom Edge Details, Granite, Kitchens, Natural Stone, Quartz, Stone Fabrication
Associations & Certifications: Better Business Bureau, Greater Houston Builders Association
Testimonials:
> Queen of the Tile is absolutely great. They did an excellent job installing my countertops. I highly recommend them.-Consumer

Every Call is Free!

DECKS

MINUTEMAN DECK AND FENCE STAINING
(877) 584-6259

In Business Since: 1999
Best At: Clean & Seal, Coating, Sealing & Finishing, Concrete Coating, Custom Staining, Deck Coating, Epoxy Coatings, Power Washing, Restoration, Sealing, Staining, Stripping, Waterproofing
Special Offers: 10% Done Right! Discount
Other Categories: Floors - Coatings, Stucco
Testimonials:

If you want an easy company to deal with you must use Minuteman Building Services. They are very nice.-Consumer

---

K & S RENOVATIONS
(877) 416-3821

In Business Since: 1995
Best At: Construction, Installation, Patios
Other Categories: Painting - Interior
Testimonials:

K & S Renovations has done a complete renovation for me. I found them to be very reliable and they have proven to do great work. I will use them again when I have another remodeling project.-Consumer

We guarantee the services
of all pros displaying the
Done Right Guarantee® logo.

DISASTER RESTORATION

ALLIED RECOVERY SERVICES
(888) 798-4680

In Business Since: 1990

Best At: 24/7 Emergency Water Extraction, Carpet & Structural Drying, Complete Restoration, Damage Restoration, Dehumidification, Duct Cleaning, Emergency Service, Flood Damage, Moisture Detection, Mold Damage Restoration, Mold Remediation, Odor Control, Residential Experts, Vapor Barriers, Water Damage, Water Extraction

Associations & Certifications: Better Business Bureau, Indoor Air Quality Association (IAQA)

Other Categories: Mold - Removal & Abatement

Testimonials:

> We've worked together for the last four years on an extensive amount of consulting on condo losses. We've also worked on $15 million worth of work for Church Mutual. Darryl is quite versatile and knowledgeable. I absolutely would recommend him.-Home Inspector

---

ADVANTAGE ENVIRONMENTAL SOLUTIONS
(800) 935-2556

In Business Since: 2001

Best At: Carpet & Structural Drying, Dehumidification, Emergency Service, Flood Damage, Mold Damage Restoration, Mold Remediation, Water Damage, Water Extraction

Associations & Certifications: American Indoor Air Quality Council Certification, Institute of Inspection, Cleaning & Restoration Certification

Other Categories: Mold - Removal & Abatement

Testimonials:

> Advantage Environmental always comes through. I trust them fully to do the work complete and to do it correctly the first time.-Consumer

---

APEX EMERGENCY SERVICES

Address: 9227 Thomasville Dr.
Houston, TX 77064

(888) 455-4889

In Business Since: 2003

Best At: 24/7 Emergency Water Extraction, Dehumidification, Sewage Spill Clean-up, Structural Drying

Associations & Certifications: Better Business Bureau

Testimonials:

> Apex Emergency Services is a fine company. They do great work and I have no hesitation in recommending their services.-Consumer

DISASTER RESTORATION CONT'D

LINDBERG SERVICES GROUP

Address: 66830 N. Eldridge Pkwy., Suite 301
Houston, TX 77041

(888) 226-3819

In Business Since: 1987
Best At: 24/7 Emergency Water Extraction, Biohazard Removal,
Dehumidification, Emergency Service, Fire Damage, Flood Damage, Mold
Remediation, Odor Control, Remodeling
Associations & Certifications: Chamber of Commerce, Institute of
Inspection, Cleaning & Restoration Certification
Testimonials:

*Lindberg Services Group is very detail orientated, professional, and fantastic to
deal with.-Consumer*

DOORS—EXTERIOR

INTERIOR DOOR CONCEPTS

Address: 9654-A Katy Fwy.
Houston, TX 77055

(877) 402-2797

In Business Since: 2005
Best At: Bi-fold Doors, Bypass, Closet Doors, Custom Wood, Decorative,
Design, French Doors, Glass, Interior Doors, Retrofits, Swinging Doors
Brands: Emtek, JELD-WEN®, Masonite®, Therma-Tru®, Yale®
Special Offers: Free door knobs with 5 or more door purchases, Referral
Program
Testimonials:

Interior Door Concepts were very professional and did a great job. I would recommend their services to anyone.-Consumer

Map & Symbols

Symbol	Area		Symbol	Area
1	Northern Suburbs		6	Western Suburbs
2	Southwest Suburbs		7	South Suburbs
3	City		A	All Areas
4	Southeast			
5	North Suburbs			

DOORS—GARAGE

PRECISION GARAGE DOOR SERVICE

 Guaranteed

Ⓐ

Address: 11875 W. Little York, #401
Houston, TX 77041

(888) 216-6048

In Business Since: 1999
Best At: Garage Door Openers, Installation, New Garage Door, Panel Replacement
Associations & Certifications: Better Business Bureau

ACME OVERHEAD DOOR COMPANY
(800) 974-9219

Guaranteed

②③⑥

In Business Since: 2005
Best At: Automatic Openers, Bent Tracks, Cables, Garage Sectionals Replaced, Installation, Overhead Doors, Service, Spring Repair, Track Repair
Special Offers: Military Discount
Associations & Certifications: Better Business Bureau
Testimonials:

Acme Overhead Door Company did an excellent job for me. They installed a new garage door for me. I would definitely use their service again.-Consumer

---

HOUSTON GARAGE DOOR PROS
(800) 838-2910

Guaranteed

②③⑥

In Business Since: 1997
Best At: Cables, Custom Wood Doors, Emergency Service, Hinges, Installation, New Garage Door, Panel Replacement, Repair, Service, Track Repair
Brands: Amarr®, Clopay®, LiftMaster®, Windsor
Testimonials:

Houston Garage Door Pros do a great job. I have nothing but good things to say about their work and their service.-Multi-unit Rental Property Owner/ Manager

Every Call is Free!

DOORS—INTERIOR

INTERIOR DOOR CONCEPTS

👍 Guaranteed

Address: 9654-A Katy Fwy.
Houston, TX 77055

Ⓐ

(877) 354-3468

In Business Since: 2005
Best At: Bi-fold Doors, Bypass, Closet Doors, Custom Wood, Decorative, Design Center, Entry Doors, European Country, French Doors, Glass, Installation, Retrofits, Sliding, Sliding & Swinging Doors, Storm, Wood
Brands: Emtek, JELD-WEN®, Masonite®, Therma-Tru®, Yale®
Special Offers: Free door knobs with 5 or more door purchases, Referral Discount

DRAIN & SEWER REPAIR

ARS/RESCUE ROOTER

👍 Guaranteed

(888) 281-6991

Ⓐ

In Business Since: 1979
License Number: M-17251
Best At: Camera Inspection, Clogs, Drain Cleaning, Drain Line Breakage, Garbage Disposals, Leak Detection, Sewer Inspection & Location, Sewer Lines & Sewer Systems, Water Lines & Pipes
Associations & Certifications: Plumbing-Heating-Cooling Contractors Association
Other Categories: Air Conditioning - Repair & Maintenance, Heating & Cooling - Repair & Maintenance

911 PLUMBING

👍 Guaranteed

(888) 843-4265

①②③⑤⑥

In Business Since: 1990
License Number: M-37412
Best At: Cable Line Cleaning, Camera Inspection, Clogs, Drain Cleaning, Emergency Service, Garbage Disposals, New Installations, Piping, Removal of Tree Roots in Pipes, Repair, Sewer Lines & Sewer Systems, Sumps
Special Offers: Discount for Done Right! Customers, Senior Citizen Discount
Testimonials:

> We use 911 Plumbing on all of our store locations plumbing needs. They show up and do the job that needs to be done.-Multi-unit Rental Property Owner/Manager

DRAPERIES

DUCT CLEANING

SEARS CARPET, UPHOLSTERY & AIR DUCT CLEANING
(877) 416-3816

In Business Since: 1995
Best At: Remove Allergens, Remove Dirt, Debris & Dust
Special Offers: Discount for Done Right! Customers
Associations & Certifications: Better Business Bureau, Carpet & Rug Institute's Gold Seal of Approval
Other Categories: Carpet - Cleaning, Emergency - Carpet Cleaning, Grout Cleaning, Tile & Stone - Cleaning, Upholstery - Cleaning & Restoration

---

MBM CLEANING
Address: 6423 Atwell Dr.
Houston, TX 77081

(888) 249-8427

In Business Since: 2000
Best At: Air Ducts, Air Filtration, Indoor Air Quality, Remove Allergens, Remove Dirt, Debris & Dust
Associations & Certifications: Better Business Bureau, Institute of Inspection, Cleaning & Restoration Certification, National Air Duct Cleaners Association (NADCA)
Testimonials:
MBM Cleaning does a tremendously clean job. -Consumer

ELECTRICIANS

For major electrical work, a licensed electrician is an absolute must.

ARS/RESCUE ROOTER
(866) 269-8883

In Business Since: 1979
License Number: 18810
Best At: Attic or Whole House Fans, Ceiling Fans, Exhaust Fans, Fixtures, Installation, Lighting, Outlets, Panel Upgrades, Switches, Thermostat Replacement, Wiring
Associations & Certifications: Plumbing-Heating-Cooling Contractors Association
Other Categories: Air Conditioning - Sales & Installation, Emergency - Electricians, Emergency - Plumbing, Heating & Cooling - Sales & Installation, Plumbing - Contractors

ELECTRICIANS CONT'D

UNIVERSAL WIRING

Address: P.O. Box 30467
Houston, TX 77249

(A)

(888) 843-4228

In Business Since: 1992
License Number: 17525
Best At: Circuit Breakers & Fuses, Dedicated Circuits, Electrical
Service Upgrades, Emergency Service, Home Re-wiring, Interior
Wiring, Lighting Design & Installation, Meter & Panel Rewires, New Home
Trouble Shooting, Outlets, Panel Upgrades, Switches, Troubleshooting
Brands: Cutler-Hammer®, HALO®, Leviton®, Lightolier®, Square D®
Special Offers: Discount for Done Right! Customers, Three Year Warranty on
All Repairs
Associations & Certifications: Better Business Bureau
Other Categories: Emergency - Electricians
Testimonials:

Ed did a great job and I would recommend him to other clients-Consumer

KENMOR ELECTRIC CO., LP

Guaranteed

Address: 8330 Hansen Rd.
Houston, TX 77075

(A)

(888) 805-8390

In Business Since: 1976
License Number: 29130
Best At: Amp Service & Amp Upgrades, Ceiling Fans, Circuit Breakers & Fuses,
Construction, Dedicated Circuits, Electrical Service Upgrades, Remodeling,
Repair, Switches, Lighting
Brands: Home Craftsman
Special Offers: 100% Satisfaction Guarantee, One Year Warranty
Associations & Certifications: American Subcontractors Association -
Houston Chapter (ASA)
Other Categories: Emergency - Electricians
Testimonials:

We guarantee the services
of all pros displaying the
Done Right Guarantee® logo.

ELECTRICIANS CONT'D

LOGO ELECTRICAL SERVICES, INC.

Address: 9506 Tallow Tree Dr.
Houston, TX 77070

(888) 841-1272

In Business Since: 2005
License Number: 23582
Best At: Aluminum Wiring, Ceiling Fans, Circuit Breakers & Fuses, Emergency Service, Home Re-wiring, Light Commercial, Lighting Design & Installation, Recessed Lighting, Service Upgrades, Troubleshooting
Special Offers: Discount for Done Right! Customers
Other Categories: Emergency - Electricians
Testimonials:
Logo Electrical Services is very reliable and professional. I highly recommend them.-General Contractor

G & A ELECTRIC CO.
(800) 970-2798

In Business Since: 1968
License Number: 11448
Best At: Additions, Bathrooms, Breakers, Computer & Phone Data Wiring, Electrical Service Upgrades, Emergency Service, Home Re-wiring, Light Commercial, Panel Upgrades, Residential Remodels
Testimonials:
G & A Electric Company has done great work for me. They are easy to work with, flexible with my schedule, prompt and reasonably priced.-Consumer

INCREDIBLE ELECTRIC

Address: P.O. Box 171
Spring, TX 77383

(888) 329-4094

In Business Since: 2003
License Number: 24677
Best At: Troubleshooting, Surge Protectors, Security Lighting, Recessed Lighting, Panel Upgrades, Outlets, Lighting Design & Installation, Emergency Service, Circuit Breakers & Fuses
Special Offers: Discount for Done Right! Customers, Free Inspection
Associations & Certifications: Better Business Bureau, Technician Seal of Safety™
Other Categories: Emergency - Electricians
Testimonials:
I've been using Albert as a subcontractor for over 6 years. He is incredibly knowledgeable and I completely trust his opinion. He does excellent work and amazes me with every job he completes. I always recommend him to anyone needing commercial or residential electrical work. -Consumer

Emergencies

EMERGENCY—CARPET CLEANING

SEARS CARPET, UPHOLSTERY & AIR DUCT CLEANING
(888) 527-9667

In Business Since: 1995
Best At: Carpet & Rug Protection, Carpet & Upholstery Cleaning, Carpet Repairs, Deep Cleaning, Deodorizing, Oriental Rugs, Stain Removal, Two-step Deep-clean Process
Special Offers: Discount for Done Right! Customers
Associations & Certifications: Better Business Bureau, Carpet & Rug Institute's Gold Seal of Approval
Other Categories: Carpet - Cleaning, Duct Cleaning, Grout Cleaning, Tile & Stone - Cleaning, Upholstery - Cleaning & Restoration

ABSOLUTE KLEEN
(888) 250-6734

In Business Since: 1981
Best At: Area Rugs, Carpet Repairs, Commercial, Deodorizing, Emergency Service, Oriental Rugs, Pet Odor Removal, Re-stretching, Stain Removal, Upholstery Cleaning
Special Offers: One Year Warranty
Associations & Certifications: Better Business Bureau
Other Categories: Carpet - Cleaning
Testimonials:

They did a great job in re-stretching my carpet. They are very experienced in what they do. I highly recommend them.-Consumer

EMERGENCY—ELECTRICIANS

ARS/RESCUE ROOTER
(888) 874-7419

In Business Since: 1979
License Number: 18810
Best At: Attic or Whole House Fans, Ceiling Fans, Exhaust Fans, Fixtures, Installation, Lighting, Outlets, Panel Upgrades, Switches, Thermostat Replacement, Wiring
Associations & Certifications: Plumbing-Heating-Cooling Contractors Association
Other Categories: Air Conditioning - Sales & Installation, Electricians, Emergency - Plumbing, Heating & Cooling - Sales & Installation, Plumbing - Contractors

EMERGENCY—ELECTRICIANS CONT'D

UNIVERSAL WIRING

Address: P.O. Box 30467
Houston, TX 77249
(866) 715-7114
In Business Since: 1992
License Number: 17525
Best At: Circuit Breakers & Fuses, Dedicated Circuits, Electrical Service Upgrades, Emergency Service, Home Re-wiring, Interior Wiring, Lighting Design & Installation, Meter & Panel Rewires, New Home Trouble Shooting, Outlets, Panel Upgrades, Switches, Troubleshooting
Brands: Cutler-Hammer®, Leviton®
Special Offers: Discount for Done Right! Customers, Three Year Warranty on All Repairs
Other Categories: Electricians
Testimonials:
Ed did a great job and I would recommend him to other clients-Consumer

KENMOR ELECTRIC CO., LP

Address: 8330 Hansen Rd.
Houston, TX 77075
(800) 854-3444
In Business Since: 1976
License Number: 29130
Best At: Amp Service & Amp Upgrades, Ceiling Fans, Circuit Breakers & Fuses, Construction, Dedicated Circuits, Electrical Service Upgrades, Lighting, Remodeling, Repair, Switches
Special Offers: 100% Satisfaction Guarantee, One Year Warranty
Other Categories: Electricians
Testimonials:

LOGO ELECTRICAL SERVICES, INC.

Address: 9506 Tallow Tree Dr.
Houston, TX 77070
(877) 374-3461
In Business Since: 2005
License Number: 23582
Best At: Aluminum Wiring, Ceiling Fans, Circuit Breakers & Fuses, Emergency Service, Home Re-wiring, Light Commercial, Lighting Design & Installation, Recessed Lighting, Service Upgrades, Troubleshooting
Special Offers: Discount for Done Right! Customers
Other Categories: Electricians
Testimonials:
Logo Electrical Services is very reliable and professional. I highly recommend them.-General Contractor

Emergencies

EMERGENCY—ELECTRICIANS CONT'D

INCREDIBLE ELECTRIC

Guaranteed

Address: P.O. Box 171
Spring, TX 77383

(800) 468-9707

In Business Since: 2003
License Number: 24677
Special Offers: Discount for Done Right! Customers, Free Inspection
Associations & Certifications: Better Business Bureau, Technician Seal of Safety™
Other Categories: Electricians
Testimonials:

I've been using Albert as a subcontractor for over 6 years. He is incredibly knowledgeable and I completely trust his opinion. He does excellent work and amazes me with every job he completes. I always recommend him to anyone needing commercial or residential electrical work. -Consumer

EMERGENCY—MAIDS

MERRY MAIDS
(888) 243-5586

Guaranteed

Ⓐ

In Business Since: 1979
Best At: Complete Home Cleaning, Housekeeping, Maid Service, Move-ins & Move-outs, Special Occasion Cleaning, Spring/Fall House Cleaning
Other Categories: Maids & Cleaning Services

Map & Symbols

① Northern Suburbs
② Southwest Suburbs
③ City
④ Southeast
⑤ North Suburbs
⑥ Western Suburbs
⑦ South Suburbs
Ⓐ All Areas

EMERGENCY—PEST CONTROL

TERMINIX
(888) 216-5794

Guaranteed Ⓐ

In Business Since: 1927
Best At: Commercial - Industrial Pest & Termite Control, Extermination, Fumigations, General Pest Control, New Home Spraying, Pest Control, Termite Control
Associations & Certifications: Better Business Bureau
Other Categories: Pest Control

HART PEST CONTROL & HORTICULTURAL SERVICES
(800) 835-9221

Guaranteed Ⓐ

In Business Since: 1969
License Number: 9001
Best At: Cockroaches, Commercial - Industrial Pest & Termite Control, Earwigs, Flea Control, General Pest Control, Hornets, New Home Spraying, Rodents, Scorpions, Silverfish, Spiders, Spot Treatment, Termite Control, Wasps
Special Offers: Free Termite Estimates, Senior Citizen Discount
Other Categories: Pest Control
Testimonials:

My company has been doing business with Hart for over 7 years. Hart handles all of my pest control needs, both professionally and personally. Corey is extremely honest, does terrific work, and is reliable. I continually recommend his services to anyone. -Consumer

EMERGENCY—PLUMBING

ARS/RESCUE ROOTER
(888) 874-7441

Guaranteed Ⓐ

In Business Since: 1979
License Number: M-17251
Best At: Complete Plumbing Needs, Faucets, Fixtures, Gas Lines, Interior Foundation Drains, Leak Detection, Piping, Sewer Lines & Sewer Systems, Sewer Main Clearing, Sump Pumps
Associations & Certifications: Plumbing-Heating-Cooling Contractors Association
Other Categories: Air Conditioning - Sales & Installation, Electricians, Emergency - Electricians, Heating & Cooling - Sales & Installation, Plumbing - Contractors

Emergencies

EMERGENCY—PLUMBING CONT'D

ABERLE PLUMBING SERVICE
(888) 407-7508

👍 **Guaranteed**

③

In Business Since: 1989
License Number: M-22759
Best At: Bathtubs, Camera Inspection, Complete Remodels, Drain Cleaning, Emergency Service, Gas Lines, Hydro Jetting, Leak Detection, Sewer Cleaning, Showers, Tankless Water Heaters, Water Heaters, Water Purifiers & Water Softeners
Associations & Certifications: Better Business Bureau
Other Categories: Plumbing - Contractors, Plumbing - Drain & Sewer
Testimonials:

We've used Aberle Plumbing for about 6-7 years now. They do very good work and I highly recommend them.-General Contractor

---

JMT PLUMBING

👍 **Guaranteed**

③

Address: P.O. Box 1771
Baytown, TX 77522

(877) 374-3471

In Business Since: 2007
License Number: M-37917
Best At: Backflows, Bathtubs, Complete Plumbing Needs, Copper Re-piping, Drain Cleaning, Emergency Service, Faucets, Fixtures, Garbage Disposals, Gas Lines, Gas Re-piping, Inspecting & Testing, Leak Repairs, Plumbing, Plumbing Rearrangements, Polybutylene Plumbing Services, Repair, Service & Maintenance, Sewer Cleaning, Showers, Sinks, Toilets, Water Drains, Water Heaters
Special Offers: Military Discount, Senior Citizen Discount
Other Categories: Plumbing - Contractors
Testimonials:

JMT Plumbing does fantastic work. I have used them on several occasions and they are always quick, clean and get the problem solved right. I highly recommend them.-Consumer

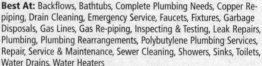

We guarantee the services
of all pros displaying the
Done Right Guarantee® logo.

EXTERMINATORS

FENCES

MINUTEMAN BUILDING SERVICES, LLC
(888) 847-0769

In Business Since: 1999
Best At: Fence & Post Damage, Wood, Wood Fencing, Fence Staining, Repair, Commercial
Special Offers: 10% Done Right! Discount
Testimonials:

If you want an easy company to deal with you must use Minuteman Building Services. They are very nice.-Consumer

BRUSHSTROKES PAINTING, INC.

Address: 17424 W. Grand Pkwy., #254
Sugar Land, TX 77479

(888) 629-3635

In Business Since: 2000
Best At: Access Control Systems, Aluminum, Animal Control, Automatic Gates, Chain Link, Colored Vinyl Fences, Commercial, Custom Fabrication, Dog Runs & Kennels, Fence & Post Damage, Installation, Iron Fencing, Ornamental Iron Work, Pool Enclosures, Railings, Residential, Commercial, & Industrial, Security & Privacy, Security Fences, Sliding, Swinging Gates, Tennis Court Enclosures, Vinyl, Wood, Wood Fencing, Wrought Iron
Associations & Certifications: Better Business Bureau
Testimonials:

We've used them as a subcontractor for the Home Depot Paint Department for the past two-and-a-half years. On a scale from 1 to 10, 10 being the highest, they would get 10's in customer service and quality of work. We've never even had a minor complaint about them.-General Contractor

BAY AREA PAINT & TILE
(877) 208-3762

In Business Since: 1985
Best At: Fence & Post Damage, Fence Staining, Installation, Security & Privacy, Security Fences, Vinyl, Wood
Special Offers: New Customer Discount
Associations & Certifications: Better Business Bureau

FIRE DAMAGE—RESTORATION

FLOOD—REPAIR & RESTORATION

FLOORS—COATINGS

MINUTEMAN BUILDING SERVICES, LLC
(877) 380-1804

Ⓐ

In Business Since: 1999
Best At: Concrete Coating, Epoxy Coatings, Garage Floor Coating, Garage Floors, Waterproofing, Paint Chip Flex Coating
Special Offers: 10% Done Right! Discount
Other Categories: Decks, Stucco
Testimonials:

If you want an easy company to deal with you must use Minuteman Building Services. They are very nice.-Consumer

We guarantee the services
of all pros displaying the
Done Right Guarantee® logo.

Every Call is Free!

FLOORS—REFINISHING & RESURFACING

FLOORS ETCETERA, INC.

Address: 1203 Roy St.
Houston, TX 77007

(800) 920-2158

In Business Since: 1992
Best At: All Woods, Coating, Sealing & Finishing, Exotics, Full Service Flooring, Hardwood Refinishing, Installation, Laminates, Maintenance Cleaning & Waxing, Pre-finished Wood, Repair, Solid & Engineered Wood Flooring, Water Damage
Brands: Anderson™, Armstrong®, Berry, Bruce®, Hartco®, Mannington®, Mohawk®, Shaw, Wilsonart®
Special Offers: Free Estimates
Associations & Certifications: Better Business Bureau, Chamber of Commerce, Greater Houston Builders Association, National Wood Flooring Association (NWFA)
Testimonials:

> We wholeheartedly recommend Floors Etcetera!. We've used their service on 3 separate occasions. Their crews are very responsive, work clean and do a really nice job.-Consumer

FLOORS—SALES & INSTALLATION

HOUSTON DESIGN CENTER

Address: 15951 FM 529, #115
Houston, TX 77095

(888) 226-8559

In Business Since: 2003
Best At: Bamboo, Ceramics, Wood, Laminates
Brands: Bruce®, Mohawk®, Quick-Step®
Special Offers: Free Estimates, Free Installation
Testimonials:

> Houston Design Center was very professional, knowledgeable and precise. I was extremely impressed with their work.-Consumer

WAYNE'S CARPET & OAK FLOORING

Address: 11633 Katy Fwy.
Houston, TX 77079

(888) 243-9340

In Business Since: 1982
Best At: Ceramic Tile, Distressed, Exotics, Hardwood, Kitchens, Laminates, Mahogany, Oak, Pre-finished Wood, Solid & Engineered Wood Flooring, Specialty Woods, Stone, Tile, Unfinished
Associations & Certifications: Better Business Bureau
Testimonials:

> Wayne's Carpet & Oak Flooring installed some hard wood flooring for me. They were very knowledgeable and did excellent work for me. I would definitely recommend their services to others.-Consumer

FLOORS—SALES & INSTALLATION CONT'D

PATTERSON CARPETS & INTERIORS, INC.

Address: 7026 Old Katy Rd., Suite 292
Houston, TX 77024

(888) 208-1702

In Business Since: 1991
Best At: Bamboo, Brazilian Cherry, Brazilian Walnut, Ceramic Tile, Engineered Wood, Hardwood Flooring, Mahogany, Marble, Natural Stone, Oak, Slate, Stone, Pre-finished Wood
Associations & Certifications: Better Business Bureau
Other Categories: Tile & Stone - Sales & Installation
Testimonials:

They do a great job. They follow through to the completion with every project I have them do.-Consumer

ART & SHOWCASE FLOORING

Address: 5200 Bellaire Blvd.
Bellaire, TX 77401

(888) 209-7196

In Business Since: 2002
Best At: Ceramic Tile, Coating, Sealing & Finishing, Hardwood, Laminates, Marble, Natural Stone, Vinyl
Brands: Anderson™, Armstrong®, Bruce®, CastleWood™, Columbia, Hartco®, Kährs, Kronoswiss®, Quick-Step®, Robbins™, Shaw®, Tarkett, Wilsonart®
Special Offers: Repeat Customer Discount
Associations & Certifications: Better Business Bureau
Testimonials:

Art & Showcase Flooring did my wood floors, carpet, counters, and tile. They did a great job and I tell Michael to bring any potential clients by so they can see the work he did.-Consumer

We guarantee the services
of all pros displaying the
Done Right Guarantee® logo.

FOUNDATION CONTRACTORS & REPAIRS

FOUNDATION SAVERS, INC.

(👍 Guaranteed)

Ⓐ

Address: 20115 FM 2100 Rd.
Crosby, TX 77532

(888) 825-1418

BBB

In Business Since: 1990
Best At: Bell Bottom Piers, Excavation, Drainage Systems
Associations & Certifications: Better Business Bureau, Chamber of Commerce, National Association of the Remodeling Industry
Testimonials:

I had a great experience dealing with Foundation Savers, Inc. They did a good job, and were very professional. -Consumer

OLSHAN FOUNDATION SOLUTIONS

(👍 Guaranteed)

Ⓐ

(877) 306-2266

BBB

In Business Since: 1933
Best At: Bell Bottom Piers, Concrete Piers, Cracked-Slab Repairs, Drainage Control, Drainage Systems, Drilled Piers, French Drains, Pier and Beam Foundations, Pressed Pilings, Retaining Walls, Root Barriers, Slab Repairs, Structural Repairs, Water Removal
Special Offers: Free Estimates, Free Inspection
Associations & Certifications: Better Business Bureau, Foundation Repair Association, Inc. (FRA)

PRECISION FOUNDATION SERVICE, INC.

(👍 Guaranteed)

Address: 8427 Hammerly Blvd.
Houston, TX 77055

(877) 346-1201

In Business Since: 1972
Best At: Bell Bottom Piers, Cracked-Slab Repairs, Engineering Inspection, Post - tension slabs, Pressed Pilings, Structural Repairs, Urethane Injections
Special Offers: Free Estimates
Associations & Certifications: Foundation Repair Association, Inc. (FRA)
Testimonials:

They are very, very good and we use them constantly. They've been with us for a long time. They do very good work and we've had no complaints. Again, they are very good and they do the job within the time frame they say they're going to do it.-Multi-unit Rental Property Owner/Manager

Every Call is Free!

FURNACE REPAIR

See Heating & Cooling—Repair & Maintenance 62

GARAGE DOORS

PRECISION GARAGE DOOR SERVICE

Guaranteed

Ⓐ

Address: 11875 W. Little York, #401
Houston, TX 77041

(888) 216-6048

In Business Since: 1999
Best At: Garage Door Openers, Installation, New Garage Door, Panel Replacement
Associations & Certifications: Better Business Bureau

BBB

We guarantee the services
of all pros displaying the
Done Right Guarantee® logo.

Map & Symbols

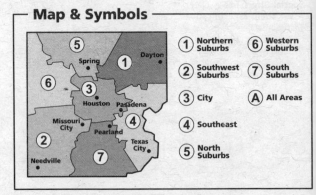

Ⓐ Spring
Dayton
① Northern Suburbs
⑥ Western Suburbs
② Southwest Suburbs
⑦ South Suburbs
③ City
Ⓐ All Areas
④ Southeast
⑤ North Suburbs

⑤
①
⑥
③
Houston
Pasadena
Missouri City
Pearland
Texas City
②
④
Needville
⑦

GARAGE DOORS CONT'D

ACME OVERHEAD DOOR COMPANY
(800) 974-9219

Guaranteed ②③⑥

In Business Since: 2005
Best At: Automatic Openers, Bent Tracks, Cables, Garage Sectionals Replaced, Installation, Overhead Doors, Service, Spring Repair, Track Repair
Special Offers: Military Discount
Associations & Certifications: Better Business Bureau
Testimonials:

Acme Overhead Door Company did an excellent job for me. They installed a new garage door for me. I would definitely use their service again.-Consumer

---

HOUSTON GARAGE DOOR PROS
(800) 838-2910

Guaranteed ②③⑥

In Business Since: 1997
Best At: Cables, Custom Wood Doors, Emergency Service, Hinges, Installation, New Garage Door, Panel Replacement, Repair, Service, Track Repair
Brands: Amarr®, Clopay®, LiftMaster®, Windsor
Testimonials:

Houston Garage Door Pros do a great job. I have nothing but good things to say about their work and their service.-Multi-unit Rental Property Owner/ Manager

GARAGE FLOORS

GRANITE

GRANITE COUNTER TOPS

GRANITE FLOORING

Every Call is Free!

GROUT CLEANING

SEARS CARPET, UPHOLSTERY & AIR DUCT CLEANING
(877) 416-3822

In Business Since: 1995
Best At: Fully Enclosed Vacuum System, High Pressure Cleaning, Sealing, Tile & Stone Grout Cleaning
Special Offers: Discount for Done Right! Customers
Associations & Certifications: Better Business Bureau, Carpet & Rug Institute's Gold Seal of Approval
Other Categories: Carpet - Cleaning, Duct Cleaning, Emergency - Carpet Cleaning, Tile & Stone - Cleaning, Upholstery - Cleaning & Restoration

MAJESTIC TILE & GROUT CLEANING, LLC
(877) 397-2486

In Business Since: 1996
Best At: Emergency Service, Fully Enclosed Vacuum System, High Pressure Cleaning, Restoration, Sealing, Stain Proof Epoxy
Testimonials:

We are an interior design company and we recommend them to all of our clients. They are very reliable. -Member of the Trade

GUTTERS & DOWNSPOUTS— INSTALLATION & REPAIR

GUTTERMAXX, LP
(800) 927-2336

In Business Since: 2002
Best At: Aluminum, Copper, Custom Fabrication, Custom Gutters, Exterior Restoration, Gutters & Downspouts, Installation, Residential & Commercial, Seamless Gutters, Storm, Water Diversion, Custom Colors, Leaf Free Gutters
Brands: K-Guard®
Special Offers: Mention Code R-5 for a Free Downspout, Mention Done Right! for Discount
Associations & Certifications: Better Business Bureau
Testimonials:

Guttermaxx did an excellent job. I would hire them again with no questions asked.-Consumer

GUTTERS & DOWNSPOUTS— INSTALLATION & REPAIR CONT'D

BISHOP GUTTER CLEANING (888) 363-2924

In Business Since: 2001
Best At: Cleaning, Leaf Screens, Leak Detection, Leak Repairs, Repair, Residential & Commercial
Testimonials:

They clean my gutters. They do a good job and I've had no complaints. I use them four times a year, once every quarter. I recommend them to anyone.- Consumer

---

GUTTER PROFESSIONALS OF GREATER HOUSTON

Address: 5829 W. Sam Houston Pkwy. N., Suite 710
Houston, TX 77041

(877) 378-8769

In Business Since: 2002
Best At: Aluminum, Copper, Custom Colors, Custom Fabrication, Custom Gutters, Custom Gutter Protection Systems, Gutters & Downspouts, Installation, Leaf Free Gutters, Seamless Gutters
Associations & Certifications: Better Business Bureau
Testimonials:

They are nothing but good. They are punctual and do what they say they're going to do. I would definitely recommend them, as I've known them for a couple of years now. -General Contractor

---

P & D GUTTERS, LLC (800) 952-0997

In Business Since: 2000
Best At: Aluminum, Cleaning, Copper, Custom Colors, Custom Fabrication, Custom Gutters, Gutters & Downspouts, Installation, Leaf Screens, Residential & Commercial, Seamless Gutters
Testimonials:

I'm a salesman for Weather Guard and he's the one that installs them for me. I don't use anyone other than Pablo. I'm really happy with him.-Member of the Trade

Every Call is Free!

HANDYMAN

HANDYMAN CONNECTION

Guaranteed

Address: 5320 Gulfton St., Suite 14
Houston, TX 77081

(877) 227-1558

In Business Since: 1993
Best At: All Home Improvement Projects, Bathrooms, Carpentry, Crown Molding, Decks, Door Repair, Doors, Dry Rot Repair, Drywall, Finish Carpentry, General Handyman, Home Improvement, Interior/Exterior Maintenance, Painting, Repair, Siding, Tile, Trim
Special Offers: Free Estimates
Associations & Certifications: Better Business Bureau
Other Categories: Carpenters

HANDYMAN MATTERS

Guaranteed

(800) 936-5448

In Business Since: 2003
Best At: Bathrooms, Cabinets, Carpentry, Counter Tops, Decks, Doors, Fencing, Flips, Framing, Basements, Drywall, Kitchens, Landscape, Painting, Roof Repair, Window Repairs
Associations & Certifications: Better Business Bureau

RDZ CONSTRUCTION

Guaranteed

Address: 5518 Ingomar Way
Houston, TX 77053

(800) 964-7993

In Business Since: 1992
Best At: Hardwood Flooring, Framing, Bathrooms, Kitchens, Painting, Brickwork, Cabinets, Concrete, Drywall, Fencing
Special Offers: Military Discount, Senior Citizen Discount
Testimonials:

> RDZ Construction has done a lot of work for us. They have always done a good job. I highly recommend them.-General Contractor

Every Call is Free!

HANDYMAN CONT'D

HOUSTON GRIME BUSTERS
(877) 248-5167

👍 Guaranteed

①②③⑤⑥

In Business Since: 2003
Best At: Bathrooms, Carpentry, Counter Tops, Decks, Doors, Drywall, Fencing, Finish Carpentry, Flooring, General Handyman, Kitchens, Painting, Pressure Washing, Trim, Window Repairs
Brands: BEHR, Deluxe, Sherwin-Williams™
Associations & Certifications: Better Business Bureau
Testimonials:

Houston Grime Busters have done an overall good job for us and I would recommend their service.-Multi-unit Rental Property Owner/Manager

GOSEN GENERAL
CONTRACTORS, INC.

👍 Guaranteed

②③⑥

Address: 10101 Southwest Freeway, Suite 315-320
Houston, TX 77074

(888) 300-1132

In Business Since: 1992
Best At: Apartment & Home Maintenance Services, Drywall, Fence Repairs, Framing, Home Improvement, Interior/Exterior Maintenance, Landscape, Lawn Maintenance, Siding, Stucco, Texture Matching, Wallpaper Removal
Associations & Certifications: Better Business Bureau
Other Categories: Carpenters

We guarantee the services
of all pros displaying the
Done Right Guarantee® logo.

H

HANDYMAN CONT'D

BAY AREA PAINT & TILE
(800) 840-4467

③④⑦

In Business Since: 1985
Best At: All Home Improvement Projects, Bathrooms, Carpentry, Finish Work, General Handyman, Installation
Special Offers: New Customer Discount
Associations & Certifications: Better Business Bureau
Other Categories: Carpenters

HARDWOOD FLOORS

HOUSTON DESIGN CENTER

Address: 15951 FM 529, #115
         Houston, TX 77095

Ⓐ

(888) 226-8559

In Business Since: 2003
Best At: Bamboo, Ceramics, Wood, Laminates
Brands: Bruce®, Mohawk®, Quick-Step®
Special Offers: Free Estimates, Free Installation
Testimonials:

Houston Design Center was very professional, knowledgeable and precise. I was extremely impressed with their work.-Consumer

WAYNE'S CARPET & OAK FLOORING

Guaranteed

Ⓐ

Address: 11633 Katy Fwy.
         Houston, TX 77079

BBB

(888) 243-9340

In Business Since: 1982
Best At: Ceramic Tile, Distressed, Exotics, Hardwood, Kitchens, Laminates, Mahogany, Oak, Pre-finished Wood, Solid & Engineered Wood Flooring, Specialty Woods, Stone, Tile, Unfinished
Associations & Certifications: Better Business Bureau
Testimonials:

Wayne's Carpet & Oak Flooring installed some hard wood flooring for me. They were very knowledgeable and did excellent work for me. I would definitely recommend their services to others.-Consumer

Every Call is Free!

HARDWOOD FLOORS CONT'D

PATTERSON CARPETS & INTERIORS, INC.

Guaranteed

②③⑥

Address: 7026 Old Katy Rd., Suite 292
Houston, TX 77024

(888) 208-1702

BBB
ACCREDITED BUSINESS

In Business Since: 1991
Best At: Bamboo, Brazilian Cherry, Brazilian Walnut, Ceramic Tile, Engineered Wood, Hardwood Flooring, Mahogany, Marble, Natural Stone, Oak, Slate, Stone, Pre-finished Wood
Associations & Certifications: Better Business Bureau
Other Categories: Tile & Stone - Sales & Installation
Testimonials:

They do a great job. They follow through to the completion with every project I have them do.-Consumer

---

ART & SHOWCASE FLOORING

Guaranteed

②③⑥

Address: 5200 Bellaire Blvd.
Bellaire, TX 77401

(888) 209-7196

BBB
ACCREDITED BUSINESS

In Business Since: 2002
Best At: Ceramic Tile, Coating, Sealing & Finishing, Hardwood, Laminates, Marble, Natural Stone, Vinyl
Brands: Anderson™, Armstrong®, Bruce®, CastleWood™, Columbia, Hartco®, Kährs, Kronoswiss®, Quick-Step®, Robbins™, Shaw®, Tarkett, Wilsonart®
Special Offers: Repeat Customer Discount
Associations & Certifications: Better Business Bureau
Testimonials:

Art & Showcase Flooring did my wood floors, carpet, counters, and tile. They did a great job and I tell Michael to bring any potential clients by so they can see the work he did.-Consumer

We guarantee the services
of all pros displaying the

Done Right Guarantee® logo.

H

The Done Right Directory

Using The Directory

How long the pro has been in business.

Guaranteed.

Areas Served.

SAMPLE LISTING

ACME SINKS & KITCHENS, INC.
123 Forest View Blvd.
Anytown, USA 12345
(800) 123-4567

👍 Guaranteed
②③④⑤⑥

In Business Since: 1990

Licenses from states and trade organizations.

License Number: 765432

Best At: Custom Door & Drawer Fronts, Custom Refacing, Laminates,

Shows you each pro's specialties quickly and easily.

Brands: Corian®, Berkeley Mills®

Any specific brands that the pro specializes in.

Special Offers: Senior Citizen Discount

Associations & Certifications: National Kitchen & Bath Association, Master Builders Association

Features offers such as free quotes and discounts.

Payment Types Accepted: American Express, Cash, Check, Discover, MasterCard, VISA

Other Categories: Remodeling - Bathrooms

Shows the pro's affiliations with trade organizations.

Indicates pro can be found in other categories.

Shows acceptable payment methods.

Done Right! Online

Visit www.DoneRight.com
to search updated listings for pros, register for the guarantee, read tips on home improvement and much more!

http://www.

The Done Right Guarantee®

(👍 Guaranteed)

Pros displaying the Done Right Guarantee logo are backed by our guarantee, which ensures that the work you asked to have done is, in fact, done right—done the way you and the Service Provider agreed it should be done. If the work you contracted for was not done right, we'll try to facilitate a good outcome for you and the Service Provider (which might include a return visit by the Service Provider). And if we can't do that, we'll either find and pay for another Service Provider to do the work right, or we'll reimburse you up to $1000.

* For details and to register for the Done Right Guarantee,
  visit www.DoneRight.com

Areas Served - Houston

Many of the home improvement pros listed serve all of Houston. Other pros list a specific area served. Please call only those pros that service your area.

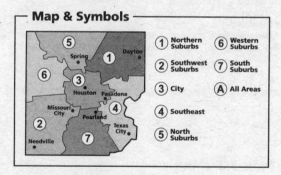

Map & Symbols

1. Northern Suburbs
2. Southwest Suburbs
3. City
4. Southeast
5. North Suburbs
6. Western Suburbs
7. South Suburbs
A. All Areas

www.DoneRight.com

HEATING & COOLING—REPAIR & MAINTENANCE

ARS/RESCUE ROOTER
(888) 731-2921

👍 Guaranteed

Ⓐ

In Business Since: 1979
License Number: TACLB00010268E
Best At: Central Air Cleaners, Central Air Conditioning, Central Humidifiers, Boilers, Forced Air Heating Systems, Furnaces, Heat Pumps, Thermostats
Associations & Certifications: Plumbing-Heating-Cooling Contractors Association
Other Categories: Air Conditioning - Repair & Maintenance, Plumbing - Drain & Sewer

---

ANDERSON HEATING
& AIR, INC.
(800) 899-1779

👍 Guaranteed

①②③⑤⑥

BBB
ACCREDITED BUSINESS

In Business Since: 1992
License Number: TACLA00006747C
Best At: Air Conditioners, Air Distribution & Air Flow, Air Filtration, Central Air, Central Heat, Energy Efficiency, Forced Air Units, Heat Pumps, Maintenance & Tune-up, Retrofits, Routine Scheduled Maintenance, Upgrades
Associations & Certifications: Better Business Bureau
Other Categories: Air Conditioning - Repair & Maintenance
Testimonials:

Anderson Heating & Air is very honest, tidy, and friendly. I have recommended their services to many people and have had no complaints whatsoever.- Consumer

Map & Symbols

① Northern Suburbs   ⑥ Western Suburbs
② Southwest Suburbs   ⑦ South Suburbs
③ City   Ⓐ All Areas
④ Southeast
⑤ North Suburbs

HEATING & COOLING—REPAIR & MAINTENANCE CONT'D

JAY'S REFRIGERATION A/C & HEATING
(888) 243-9347

In Business Since: 1993
License Number: TACLB00013930E
Best At: All Brands & Models, Compressors, Emergency Service, Energy Efficiency, Forced Air Units, Heat Pumps, Maintenance & Tune-up, Replacement, Humidifiers & Dehumidifiers, Thermostats, Service
Brands: American Standard, Ruud®, Trane®
Other Categories: Air Conditioning - Repair & Maintenance
Testimonials:

I have done business with Jay's Refrigeration for some time now. He is very reliable, and does terrific work. I recommend him every chance I get.-Consumer

---

SUNBELT AIR CONDITIONING & HEATING

Address: 7407 Shady Vale Ln.
Houston, TX 77040

(888) 841-1242

In Business Since: 1992
License Number: TACLB00010628E
Best At: Air Ducts, Air Distribution & Air Flow, Air Conditioning, Central Heat, Compressors, Emergency Service, Forced Air Units, Replacement, Upgrades, Air Filtration
Brands: American Standard, Carrier®, Frigidaire®, Goodman®
Special Offers: 6 Month Warranty On Repairs, One Year Warranty on Installation
Associations & Certifications: Better Business Bureau
Other Categories: Air Conditioning - Repair & Maintenance
Testimonials:

We have been using Sunbelt for over 14 years. They always do great work and have yet to be under-bid for any job we have had for them. We have and will continue to recommend them to anyone needing their services.-Realtor

---

SEARS HOME SERVICES
(877) 201-3317

In Business Since: 1906
License Number: TACLB00019160E
Best At: Air Conditioning, All Brands & Models, Central Air, Central Air Cleaners, Central Air Conditioning, Central Heat, Central Humidifiers, Forced Air Heating Systems, Forced Air Units, Furnaces, Gas Heat & Oil Heat, Geothermal Heating & Cooling Systems, Heat Pumps, Heaters, Heating, Maintenance & Tune-up, Preventative Maintenance, Replacement, Service, Thermostats
Brands: Carrier®, Heil®, Kenmore®, Tempstar®, Trane®
Special Offers: Pre-Season Tune-Up Specials
Associations & Certifications: Better Business Bureau, ENERGY STAR

HEATING & COOLING—SALES & INSTALLATION

ARS/RESCUE ROOTER
(888) 791-4103

👍 Guaranteed
Ⓐ

In Business Since: 1979
License Number: TACLB00010268E
Best At: Central Air Cleaners, Central Air Conditioning, Central Humidifiers, Forced Air Heating Systems, Heat Pumps, Thermostat Replace or Reprogram
Associations & Certifications: Plumbing-Heating-Cooling Contractors Association
Other Categories: Air Conditioning - Sales & Installation, Electricians, Emergency - Electricians, Emergency - Plumbing, Plumbing - Contractors

---

SEARS HOME
IMPROVEMENT PRODUCTS
(877) 334-8554

👍 Guaranteed
Ⓐ

BBB ACCREDITED BUSINESS bbb.org

In Business Since: 1984
License Number: TACLB00019160E
Best At: Air Conditioners, Boilers, Central Air, Central Heat, Energy Efficiency, Furnaces, Heat Pumps
Brands: Carrier®, Kenmore®
Special Offers: Free Estimates
Associations & Certifications: Better Business Bureau, ENERGY STAR
Other Categories: Air Conditioning - Sales & Installation

ANDERSON HEATING
& AIR, INC.
(800) 735-1194

👍 Guaranteed

BBB ACCREDITED BUSINESS bbb.org

In Business Since: 1992
License Number: TACLA00006747C
Best At: Air Conditioning, Air Distribution & Air Flow, Air Filtration, Central Air, Central Heat, Custom Indoor Comfort System, Designing HVAC Systems, Energy Efficiency, Forced Air Units, Heat Pumps, Retrofits, Upgrades
Associations & Certifications: Better Business Bureau
Other Categories: Air Conditioning - Sales & Installation
Testimonials:

Anderson Heating & Air is very honest, tidy, and friendly. I have recommended their services to many people and had no complaints whatsoever.-Consumer

Every Call is Free!

HEATING & COOLING—SALES & INSTALLATION CONT'D

JAY'S REFRIGERATION A/C & HEATING
(888) 249-1887

👍 Guaranteed

②③⑥

In Business Since: 1993
License Number: TACLB00013930E
Best At: Air Balancing, Air Cleaners, Air Conditioners, Air Conditioning, Air Distribution & Air Flow, Air Ducts, Air Filtration, Air Purification, Air Quality Testing, Central Air, Central Heat
Brands: American Standard, Ruud®, Trane®
Other Categories: Air Conditioning - Sales & Installation
Testimonials:

I have done business with Jay's Refrigeration for some time now. He is very reliable and does terrific work. I recommend him every chance I get.-Consumer

SUNBELT AIR CONDITIONING & HEATING

👍 Guaranteed

③

Address: 7407 Shady Vale Ln.
Houston, TX 77040

(888) 234-3121

BBB
ACCREDITED
BUSINESS

In Business Since: 1992
License Number: TACLB00010628E
Best At: Air Balancing, Air-ready Add-ons, All Major Brands, Central Air Conditioning, Central Heat, Central Humidifiers, Comfort Heat Technology, Compressors, Designing HVAC Systems, Energy Efficiency, Heat Pumps, Humidifiers & Dehumidifiers, Inspecting & Testing, Replacement, Upgrades, Warranties
Special Offers: 6 Month Warranty On Repairs, One Year Warranty on Installation
Associations & Certifications: Better Business Bureau
Testimonials:

We have been using Sunbelt for over 14 years. They always do great work and have yet to be under-bid for any job we have had for them. We have and will continue to recommend them to anyone needing their services..-Realtor

We guarantee the services
of all pros displaying the
Done Right Guarantee® logo.

H

BAD PROS ARE NOT ALLOWED AT DONE RIGHT!

If you have a bad experience with one of our pros,

Contact us at
1-800-494-6005 - Option 2

or via email at
Trouble@DoneRight.com.

We will always help.

HOME THEATER—SALES, INSTALLATION & REPAIR

FRONT & CENTER TECHNOLOGIES, INC.
(866) 594-7774

(A)

In Business Since: 2002
Best At: All Size Jobs, Custom Installations, Custom Work, Design, Entire Homes, Home Automation, Home Theater Design, Media Centers, Multimedia Servers, Networking, Video Surveillance, Retrofits
Brands: Crestron®, Da-Lite®, DENON, Harman Kardon®, JVC®, NEC Electronics, Panasonic, Pioneer, Polk Audio®, Proficient Audio Systems, Russound®, Sharp®, Sony®, Universal® Remote Control, Yamaha
Associations & Certifications: National Systems Contractors Association (NSCA)
Testimonials:

We've used Front & Center as a sub-contractor for several years. They are timely, consistent, have good customer service, and produce good, clean work.-Member of the Trade

INSULATION

PAYLESS INSULATION
Address: 1331 Seamist Dr.
Houston, TX 77008
(866) 342-1776

In Business Since: 1979
Best At: Blown-in Insulation, New Homes, Retrofits, Spray-ons, Cotton
Brands: Celbar®, International Cellulose, UltraTouch
Associations & Certifications: Better Business Bureau, Insulation Contractors Association of America (ICAA)
Testimonials:

Payless Insulation always comes through with any of our many projects. They are very, very good.-Multi-unit Rental Property Owner/Manager

We guarantee the services
of all pros displaying the
Done Right Guarantee® logo.

INSULATION CONT'D

ALL-TECH INSULATION SERVICES, INC.

👍 **Guaranteed**

③④⑦

Address: 1500 Marina Bay Dr., Suite 3530
Kemah, TX 77565

(877) 444-3373

BBB ACCREDITED BUSINESS

In Business Since: 2002
Best At: Attic Fans, Blown-in Insulation, Insulation Removal, New Homes, Retrofits, Ventilation
Brands: CertainTeed, Johns Manville, Knauf Insulation, Owens Corning®
Special Offers: Military Discount, Referral Discount, Senior Citizen Discount, Winter Discount
Associations & Certifications: Better Business Bureau, Insulation Contractors Association of America (ICAA)
Testimonials:
They installed some blown insulation. They did a great job. Everything was fine.-Consumer

KITCHEN REMODELING

SEARS HOME IMPROVEMENT PRODUCTS
(877) 329-6812

👍 **Guaranteed**

Ⓐ

BBB ACCREDITED BUSINESS

In Business Since: 1984
Best At: 100s of Drawer & Cabinet Styles & Colors, Cabinets, Counter Tops, Custom Cabinet Refacing, Hardware, Match any Styles, Sinks, Turnkey Installation
Brands: Aristokraft®, Corian®, DuPont™, Zodiaq®
Special Offers: Free Estimates
Associations & Certifications: Better Business Bureau, ENERGY STAR, Texas Residential Construction Commission

We guarantee the services
of all pros displaying the
Done Right Guarantee® logo.

KITCHEN REMODELING CONT'D

FLOOR COVERINGS & MORE, INC.

Guaranteed

(A)

Address: 2395 Highway 6 South, Suite F
Houston, TX 77077

(800) 840-1193

In Business Since: 1989
Best At: Additions, Cabinet Refacing, Cabinets, Carpentry, Complete Remodels, Counter Tops, Custom Cabinets, Flooring, Painting
Brands: Daltile®, Emser Tile®, KraftMaid, Mannington®, Pergo®, Quick-Step®
Special Offers: Two Year Financing with No Interest
Associations & Certifications: Texas Residential Construction Commission
Other Categories: Remodeling - Bathrooms
Testimonials:

I highly recommend Floor Coverings & More. They are very friendly and easy to deal with.-Consumer

---

LARR-WOOD CONSTRUCTION

Guaranteed

①②③⑤⑥

Address: 19515 Wied Rd., Suite B
Spring, TX 77388

(888) 893-9288

In Business Since: 2001
Best At: Additions, Cabinets, Complete Remodels, Counter Tops, Flooring, Repair, Restoration
Special Offers: Satisfaction Guarantee
Associations & Certifications: Texas Residential Construction Commission
Other Categories: Remodeling - Bathrooms
Testimonials:

I've used Larr-Wood for over 6 years now. All I can say is that Larry has the most professional and reliable company. His crew does excellent work, and I have recommended Larr-Wood to everyone who needed his services.-General Contractor

LAWN CARE

TRUGREEN
(888) 595-0006

Guaranteed

(A)

In Business Since: 1979
Best At: Aerating, Fertilizing, Lawn Pests, Weed Control
Associations & Certifications: Better Business Bureau

LEAK DETECTION

See Plumbing—Contractors. 82

MAIDS & CLEANING SERVICES

MERRY MAIDS
(888) 798-4678

👍 Guaranteed

(A)

In Business Since: 1979
Best At: Complete Home Cleaning, Housekeeping, Maid Service, Move-ins &
Move-outs, Special Occasion Cleaning, Spring/Fall House Cleaning
Other Categories: Emergency - Maids

MAID BRIGADE
(800) 889-5190

👍 Guaranteed

🌲 Green Merchant

(1)(3)(4)(5)(7)

In Business Since: 1979
Best At: Bathrooms, Bi-weekly, Common Area,
Complete Home Cleaning, Kitchens, Monthly, Move-ins
& Move-outs, Weekly
Associations & Certifications: Green Clean Certification

HOLY MAID
(877) 257-2909

👍 Guaranteed

(3)

In Business Since: 2005
Best At: All Living Areas, Bathrooms, Bedrooms, Carpet Cleaning, Floors,
Kitchens, Mirrors, Remove Clutter, Trash, Vacuuming
Testimonials:

*Holy Maid has been cleaning for a while now. They are prompt, never miss an
appointment and do a very nice job.-General Contractor*

Map & Symbols

(1)	Northern Suburbs	(6)	Western Suburbs
(2)	Southwest Suburbs	(7)	South Suburbs
(3)	City	(A)	All Areas
(4)	Southeast		
(5)	North Suburbs		

MARBLE

MOLD—INSPECTION

ALLIED RECOVERY SERVICES
(888) 795-9991

In Business Since: 1990
Best At: Clean-up Planning, Drainage Systems, Emergency Service, Flood Damage, Independent Assessment, Indoor Air Quality, Infrared Camera Moisture Detection, Lab Testing, Leak Detection, Moisture Measurement, Mold & Mildew Odor Control, Toxic Black Mold Discovery, Vapor Barriers, Ventilation, Visual Assessment, Water Extraction, Written Remediation Procedure
Associations & Certifications: Better Business Bureau, Indoor Air Quality Association (IAQA)
Testimonials:

> We've worked together for the last four years on an extensive amount of consulting on condo losses. We've also worked on $15 million worth of work for Church Mutual. Darryl is quite versatile and knowledgeable. I absolutely would recommend him. -Home Inspector

GUARDIAN ENVIRONMENTAL
(800) 935-1884

In Business Since: 1990
Best At: Clean-up Planning, Detection, Emergency Service, Independent Assessment, Visual Assessment, Written Remediation Procedure
Testimonials:

> I've known Tom at Guardian Environmental for about 16 years now. He has done all of the inspections for various investment and commercial properties for me. He is an honest man with an excellent work ethic.-Consumer

MCKEE ENVIRONMENTAL
HEALTH, INC.

Address: 303 Westfield Ln.
Friendswood, TX 77546

(800) 948-2331

In Business Since: 1982
Best At: Independent Assessment, Leak Detection, Moisture Detection, Toxic Black Mold Discovery
Associations & Certifications: Better Business Bureau
Testimonials:

> It was a good experience. They did a good job. The report was very detailed. The cost was way better than their competitors.-Consumer

MOLD

MOLD—REMOVAL & ABATEMENT

ALLIED RECOVERY SERVICES
(888) 801-7136

In Business Since: 1990
Best At: Allergens, Biohazard Removal, Dehumidification, Detection, Drainage Systems, Emergency Service, Flood Damage, Infrared Camera Moisture Detection, Inspections, Leak Detection, Moisture Detection, Mold & Mildew Testing, Mold Damage Restoration, Structural Drying, Toxic Black Mold Discovery, Vapor Barriers, Ventilation, Water Damage, Water Extraction
Associations & Certifications: Better Business Bureau, Indoor Air Quality Association (IAQA)
Other Categories: Water & Fire Damage - Repair & Restoration
Testimonials:

> We've worked together for the last four years on an extensive amount of consulting on condo losses. We've also worked on $15 million worth of work for Church Mutual. Darryl is quite versatile and knowledgeable. I absolutely would recommend him.-Home Inspector

---

ADVANTAGE ENVIRONMENTAL
SOLUTIONS
(877) 452-4478

In Business Since: 2001
Best At: Carpet & Structural Drying, Dehumidification, Duct Cleaning, Emergency Service, Flood Damage, Moisture Detection, Mold Damage Restoration, Mold Remediation, Water Damage, Water Extraction
Other Categories: Water & Fire Damage - Repair & Restoration
Testimonials:

> Advantage Environmental always comes through. I trust them fully to do the work complete and to do it correctly the first time.-Consumer

---

ARC CONSTRUCTION
(800) 939-0771

In Business Since: 1986
Best At: Allergens, Carpet & Structural Drying, Dehumidification, Drainage Systems, Duct Cleaning, Emergency Service, Flood Damage, Mold & Mildew Odor Control, Mold Damage Restoration, Mold Remediation, No Inspections
Associations & Certifications: Better Business Bureau
Testimonials:

> I've had a professional relationship with ARC Construction for about 7 years now. It has been my experience that ARC does an excellent job.-Consumer

PAINTING—EXTERIOR

TURNKEY PAINTING, INC.

👍 Guaranteed

Address: 10422 Rockley Rd.
Houston, TX 77099

Ⓐ

(888) 234-3105

In Business Since: 1992

Best At: Brush, Color Matching, Complete Home Painting Interior
and/or Exterior, Deck & Siding Staining, Faux Finishing, Premium
Quality Paint, Textures, Trim, Whole House Painting, Wood Finishing

Brands: PPG/Monarch Paint, Sherwin-Williams™

Associations & Certifications: Better Business Bureau

Testimonials:

> Turnkey Painting proved to be dependable and I liked that they kept me updated
> on their progress. I would use their services again.-Consumer

---

CERTAPRO PAINTERS
(800) 889-6536

👍 Guaranteed

In Business Since: 1992

Best At: Complimentary Color Consultation, Consultation with
Experienced Estimator, Premium Quality Paint, Radiant Barrier Paint,
Final Clean-up & Inspection

Brands: Sherwin-Williams™

Associations & Certifications: Better Business Bureau, Chamber
of Commerce

Other Categories: Painting - Interior

M

P

BRUSHSTROKES PAINTING, INC.

👍 Guaranteed

Address: 17424 W. Grand Pkwy., #254
Sugar Land, TX 77479

Ⓐ

(888) 839-0218

In Business Since: 2000

Best At: Color Consultation, Color Matching, Complete Home
Painting Interior and/or Exterior, Consultation with Experienced
Estimator, Custom Colors, Deck & Siding Staining, Premium Quality
Paint, Protective Coatings & Protective Sealants, Top Quality Preparation, Trim
Finishes, Whole House Painting

Associations & Certifications: Better Business Bureau

Testimonials:

> We've used them as a subcontractor for the Home Depot Paint Department for
> the past two-and-a-half years. On a scale from 1 to 10, 10 being the highest,
> they would get 10's in customer service and quality of work. We've never even
> had a minor complaint about them.-General Contractor

Every Call is Free!

PAINTING—EXTERIOR CONT'D

K & S RENOVATIONS
(888) 213-6612

Guaranteed

(A)

In Business Since: 1995
Best At: Brush, Color Consultation, Complete Home Painting Interior and/or Exterior, Clean Drop Cloths
Associations & Certifications: Better Business Bureau, Texas Residential Construction Commission
Testimonials:

K & S Renovations has done a complete renovation for me. I found them to be very reliable and they have proven to do great work. I will use them again when I have another remodeling project.-Consumer

PRO PAINTERS

Guaranteed

(3)(4)(7)

Address: 12430 Galveston Rd., Unit B-17
Webster, TX 77598

(888) 225-1409

In Business Since: 1995
Best At: Brush, Color Consultation, Color Matching, Consultation with Experienced Estimator, Custom Colors, Deck & Siding Staining, Exterior Restoration, Power Washing, Premium Quality Paint, Protective Coatings & Protective Sealants, Top Quality Preparation, Whole House Painting
Associations & Certifications: Better Business Bureau
Testimonials:

Pro Painters is a good company to work with. They stay on top of things and do a good job of communicating with us.-General Contractor

GOSEN GENERAL
CONTRACTORS, INC.

Guaranteed

(2)(3)(6)

Address: 10101 Southwest Freeway, Suite 315-320
Houston, TX 77074

(800) 297-3028

In Business Since: 1992
Best At: Carpentry, Caulking, Color Matching, Complete Home Painting Interior and/or Exterior, Complimentary Color Consultation, Faux Finishing, Power Washing, Refinishing, Repainting, Restoration, Staining, Textures, Walls
Brands: Benjamin Moore®, ICI Paints, Pittsburgh®, Sherwin-Williams™
Associations & Certifications: Better Business Bureau
Testimonials:

We've used Gosen General on several occasions, and we are always happy with their quality of work.-General Contractor

Every Call is Free!

PAINTING—INTERIOR

BRUSHSTROKES PAINTING, INC. 👍 Guaranteed

Address: 17424 W. Grand Pkwy., #254
Sugar Land, TX 77479　Ⓐ

(888) 835-6784

In Business Since: 2000
Best At: Accent Colors, Brush, Color Consultation, Color Matching, Complete Home Painting Interior and/or Exterior, Consultation with Experienced Estimator, Custom Colors, Faux Finishing, Oil Base Woodwork, Premium Quality Paint, Repainting, Whole House Painting
Associations & Certifications: Better Business Bureau
Testimonials:

We've used them as a subcontractor for the Home Depot Paint Department for the past two-and-a-half years. On a scale from 1 to 10, 10 being the highest, they would get 10's in customer service and quality of work. We've never even had a minor complaint about them.-General Contractor

BAY AREA PAINT & TILE 👍 Guaranteed
(877) 451-5264　①③④⑦

In Business Since: 1985
Best At: Brush, Color Consultation, Color Matching, Complete Home Painting Interior and/or Exterior, Custom Interior, Staining, Textures
Special Offers: New Customer Discount
Other Categories: Tile & Stone - Sales & Installation

CERTAPRO PAINTERS 👍 Guaranteed
(800) 889-6536　①②③⑤⑥

In Business Since: 1992
Best At: Complimentary Color Consultation, Consultation with Experienced Estimator, Final Clean-up & Inspection, Furniture Protection, Premium Quality Paint, Site Preparation
Brands: Sherwin-Williams™
Associations & Certifications: Better Business Bureau, Chamber of Commerce
Other Categories: Painting - Exterior

P

We guarantee the services
of all pros displaying the
Done Right Guarantee® logo.

PAINTING—INTERIOR CONT'D

K & S RENOVATIONS
(888) 214-4938

👍 Guaranteed

Ⓐ

In Business Since: 1995
Best At: Brush, Clean Drop Cloths, Color Consultation, Complete
Home Painting Interior and/or Exterior
Associations & Certifications: Better Business Bureau, Texas
Residential Construction Commission
Other Categories: Decks
Testimonials:

*K & S Renovations has done a complete renovation for me. I found them to
be very reliable and they have proven to do great work. I will use them again
when I have another remodeling project.-Consumer*

MCCAIN KITCHEN & BATH
Address: 9815 Hughes Ranch Rd.
Houston, TX 77089

(800) 934-1339

👍 Guaranteed

Ⓐ

In Business Since: 1981
Best At: Brush, Color Matching, Consultation, Cracks, Final Clean-up &
Inspection, Premium Coating
Testimonials:

*I was very pleased with the work McCain Kitchen & Bath did for me. I highly
recommend them.-Consumer*

PAINTING—INTERIOR CONT'D

GOSEN GENERAL CONTRACTORS, INC.

Address: 10101 Southwest Freeway, Suite 315-320
Houston, TX 77074

(888) 878-8056

In Business Since: 1992
Best At: Cabinets, Carpentry, Caulking, Ceilings, Color Matching, Custom Work, Doors, Faux Finishing, Repainting, Staining, Textures, Whole House Painting
Brands: Benjamin Moore®, ICI Paints, Pittsburgh®, Sherwin-Williams™
Associations & Certifications: Better Business Bureau
Other Categories: Tile & Stone - Sales & Installation
Testimonials:

We've used Gosen General on several occasions, and we are always happy with their quality of work.-General Contractor

---

TURNKEY PAINTING, INC.

Address: 10422 Rockley Rd.
Houston, TX 77099

(888) 242-9307

In Business Since: 1992
Best At: Brush, Color Matching, Complete Home Painting Interior and/or Exterior, Crown Moldings, Faux Finishing, Interior & Exterior, Premium Quality Paint, Residential & Commercial, Textures, Trim, Walls, Whole House Painting, Wood Trim
Brands: PPG/Monarch Paint, Sherwin-Williams™
Associations & Certifications: Better Business Bureau
Testimonials:

Turnkey Painting proved to be dependable and I liked that they kept me updated on their progress. I would use their services again.-Consumer

Every Call is Free!

PATIO, PORCHES & ENCLOSURES

ADVANCE PRODUCTS & CONSTRUCTION

👍 Guaranteed

Ⓐ

Address: 8610 Brookcrest Cir.
Houston, TX 77072

(800) 961-8996

In Business Since: 1979

Best At: Custom Design, Patio Covers, Patio Rooms, Pool Enclosures, Replacement Windows & Doors, Sunrooms & Solariums, Insulated Patio Covers, Pergolas, Screen Enclosures

Associations & Certifications: Better Business Bureau

Testimonials:

Fantastic! The project came out just as we hoped for and more.-Consumer

BBB ACCREDITED BUSINESS

FIVE STAR HOUSE PAINTING, INC.
(877) 387-3674

👍 Guaranteed

②③⑥

In Business Since: 1994

Best At: Concrete, Custom Design, Custom Patio Covers, Decks, Gazebos, Indoor, New Builds, Outdoor, Painting, Patio Covers, Patio Enclosures, Renovation, Rooms, Siding, Slabs, Walkways

Brands: James Hardie®

Special Offers: Free Estimates, Holiday Discount

Associations & Certifications: Better Business Bureau, Texas Residential Construction Commission

Testimonials:

They've done a lot of remodeling for our church. They do a fantastic job. They are extremely affordable and have great customer service. I couldn't say enough good stuff about them. 100%, I absolutely recommend them.-Consumer

BBB ACCREDITED BUSINESS

Map & Symbols

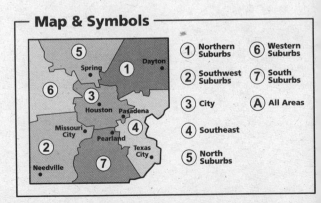

① Northern Suburbs	⑥ Western Suburbs
② Southwest Suburbs	⑦ South Suburbs
③ City	Ⓐ All Areas
④ Southeast	
⑤ North Suburbs	

PEST CONTROL

TERMINIX
(888) 724-1220

Guaranteed

Ⓐ

In Business Since: 1927
Best At: Extermination, Fumigations, Pest Control, Termite Control, Commercial - Industrial Pest & Termite Control, General Pest Control, New Home Spraying
Associations & Certifications: Better Business Bureau
Other Categories: Emergency - Pest Control

HART PEST CONTROL & HORTICULTURAL SERVICES
(888) 273-4471

Guaranteed

Ⓐ

In Business Since: 1969
License Number: 9001
Best At: Commercial - Industrial Pest & Termite Control, General Pest Control, Rodents, Spot Treatment, Termite Control, Cockroaches, Earwigs, Flea Control, Hornets, New Home Spraying, Scorpions, Silverfish, Spiders, Wasps
Special Offers: Free Termite Estimates, Senior Citizen Discount
Associations & Certifications: Better Business Bureau
Other Categories: Emergency - Pest Control
Testimonials:

My company has been doing business with Hart for over 7 years. Hart handles all of my pest control needs, both professionally and personally. Corey is extremely honest, does terrific work, and is reliable. I continually recommend his services to anyone. -Consumer

---

NATURE'S PEST SOLUTIONS
Address: 1715 W. 22nd St.
Houston, TX 77008

(888) 801-7137

Guaranteed

Ⓐ

In Business Since: 2006
License Number: 13430
Best At: Commercial - Industrial Pest & Termite Control, Extermination, Flea Control, Interiors, Mosquitoes, New Home Spraying, Opossums, Pest Control, Raccoons, Rats, Rodents
Special Offers: Discount for Done Right! Customers
Associations & Certifications: Greater Houston Builders Association
Testimonials:

We've used Nature's Pest Solution's for over 1 year now and they have done excellent work for us. I refer their services to others frequently.-Consumer

Every Call is Free!

BAD PROS ARE NOT ALLOWED AT DONE RIGHT!

If you have a bad experience with one of our pros,

Contact us at
1-800-494-6005 - Option 2

or via email at
Trouble@DoneRight.com.

We will always help.

PLUMBING—BATHTUBS & SINKS— REPAIR & REFINISH

911 PLUMBING
(888) 843-4251

👍 Guaranteed
① ② ③ ⑤ ⑥

In Business Since: 1990
License Number: M-37412
Best At: Bathtubs, Hydro Cleaning, Parts, Sinks, Wash Basins
Special Offers: Discount for Done Right! Customers, Senior Citizen Discount
Testimonials:

We use 911 Plumbing on all of our store locations plumbing needs. They show up and do the job that needs to be done.-Multi-unit Rental Property Owner/ Manager

TUBS & TOPS
(888) 610-1009

👍 Guaranteed
Ⓐ

In Business Since: 1986
Best At: Bathtubs, Fixture Resurfacing, Porcelain, Porcelain Chip Repair, Sinks, Wash Basins
Testimonials:

Tubs and Tops has done a few jobs for us. They have repaired and resurfaced tubs for us, as well as resurfaced some counter tops. I would definitely recommend their services to others.-Consumer

P

We guarantee the services
of all pros displaying the
Done Right Guarantee® logo.

PLUMBING—CONTRACTORS

For major plumbing work, a licensed Plumbing
Contractor is an absolute must.

ARS/RESCUE ROOTER
(888) 422-1794
In Business Since: 1979
License Number: M-17251
Best At: Complete Plumbing Needs, Faucets, Fixtures, Gas Lines, Interior Foundation Drains, Leak Detection, Piping, Sewer Lines & Sewer Systems, Sewer Main Clearing, Sump Pumps
Brands: American Standard, Delta®, GROHE, Kohler®, Moen®, TOTO®
Associations & Certifications: Plumbing-Heating-Cooling Contractors Association
Other Categories: Air Conditioning - Sales & Installation, Electricians, Emergency - Electricians, Emergency - Plumbing, Heating & Cooling - Sales & Installation

👍 Guaranteed
(A)

SOUTHERN PLUMBING
SERVICES, LLC
Address: 11806 Ainsworth Dr.
Stafford, TX 77477
(877) 315-3914
In Business Since: 2004
License Number: M - 36796
Best At: Cable Line Cleaning, Camera Inspection, Complete Plumbing Needs, Emergency Service, Epoxy Pipe Lining, Fixtures, Gas Lines, Piping, Re-route, Repair, Sewer Cleaning, Sewer Damage, Tankless Water Heaters, Water Heaters, Water Lines & Pipes
Testimonials:

Southern Plumbing Services has been providing service to us for the last 4-5 years. We continue to be happy with their service and the quality of their work.-General Contractor

👍 Guaranteed
(A)

We guarantee the services
of all pros displaying the
Done Right Guarantee® logo.

PLUMBING—CONTRACTORS CONT'D

ABERLE PLUMBING SERVICE
(877) 400-7998

(3)

In Business Since: 1989
License Number: M-22759
Best At: Bathtubs, Camera Inspection, Complete Remodels, Drain Cleaning, Gas Lines, Hydro Jetting, Leak Detection, Sewer Cleaning, Showers, Tankless Water Heaters, Water Heaters, Water Purifiers & Water Softeners
Associations & Certifications: Better Business Bureau
Other Categories: Emergency - Plumbing
Testimonials:

> We've used Aberle Plumbing for about 6-7 years now. They do very good work and I highly recommend them.-General Contractor

---

JMT PLUMBING
Address: P.O. Box 1771
Baytown, TX 77522

(888) 739-1817

(3)

In Business Since: 2007
License Number: M-37917
Best At: Backflows, Bathtubs, Complete Plumbing Needs, Copper Re-piping, Drain Cleaning, Emergency Service, Faucets, Fixtures, Garbage Disposals, Gas Lines, Gas Re-piping, Inspecting & Testing, Leak Repairs, Plumbing, Plumbing Rearrangements, Polybutylene Plumbing Services, Repair, Service & Maintenance, Water Heaters, Sewer Cleaning, Showers, Sinks, Toilets, Water Drains
Special Offers: Military Discount, Senior Citizen Discount
Other Categories: Emergency - Plumbing
Testimonials:

> JMT Plumbing does fantastic work. I have used them on several occasions and they are always quick, clean and get the problem solved right. I highly recommend them.-Consumer

Every Call is Free!

PLUMBING—DRAIN & SEWER

ARS/RESCUE ROOTER
(888) 281-6991

👍 Guaranteed

Ⓐ

In Business Since: 1979
License Number: M-17251
Best At: Camera Inspection, Clogs, Drain Cleaning, Drain Line Breakage, Garbage Disposals, Leak Detection, Sewer Inspection & Location, Sewer Lines & Sewer Systems, Water Lines & Pipes
Associations & Certifications: Plumbing-Heating-Cooling Contractors Association
Other Categories: Air Conditioning - Repair & Maintenance, Heating & Cooling - Repair & Maintenance

911 PLUMBING
(888) 843-4265

👍 Guaranteed

①②③⑤⑥

In Business Since: 1990
License Number: M-37412
Best At: Cable Line Cleaning, Camera Inspection, Clogs, Drain Cleaning, Emergency Service, Garbage Disposals, New Installations, Piping, Removal of Tree Roots in Pipes, Repair, Sewer Lines & Sewer Systems, Sumps
Special Offers: Discount for Done Right! Customers, Senior Citizen Discount
Testimonials:

> We use 911 Plumbing on all of our store locations plumbing needs. They show up and do the job that needs to be done.-Multi-unit Rental Property Owner/ Manager

We guarantee the services
of all pros displaying the
Done Right Guarantee® logo.

PLUMBING—FIXTURES

ARS/RESCUE ROOTER
(888) 219-8195

👍 **Guaranteed**

Ⓐ

In Business Since: 1979
License Number: M-17251
Best At: Faucets, Garbage Disposals, Installation, Piping, Repair, Showers, Sinks, Toilets, Tubs
Brands: American Standard, Delta®, GROHE, Kohler®, Moen®, TOTO®
Associations & Certifications: Plumbing-Heating-Cooling Contractors Association

PLUMBING—WATER HEATERS

911 PLUMBING
(888) 843-4412

👍 **Guaranteed**

①②③⑤⑥

In Business Since: 1990
License Number: M-37412
Best At: Emergency Service, Gas Lines, Inspecting & Testing, Installation, Leak Repairs, New Installations, Piping, Preventative Maintenance, Re-piping, Repair, Service & Maintenance, Tankless Water Heaters
Special Offers: Discount for Done Right! Customers, Senior Citizen Discount
Testimonials:

We use 911 Plumbing on all of our store locations plumbing needs. They show up and do the job that needs to be done.-Multi-unit Rental Property Owner/ Manager

P

POOLS & SPAS—CONTRACTORS & NEW BUILDS

CREATIVE LIFESTYLE POOLS
(888) 841-1132

👍 **Guaranteed**

Ⓐ

In Business Since: 1973
Best At: Concrete, Custom Pools, Custom Waterfalls
Testimonials:

I have done business with Creative Lifestyle Pools for about 5 years. Jim is a great person to work with, and he always does a superb job. -General Contractor

Every Call is Free!

PRESSURE WASHING

KDS SERVICES, INC.
👍 Guaranteed

(888) 866-7689
Ⓐ

In Business Since: 1995
Best At: Driveways, Fencing, Home Exteriors, Patios, Sidewalks, Curbs, Pool Decks, Wood Decks
Special Offers: Mention Done Right! for a Special Offer
Associations & Certifications: Texas Commission on Environmental Quality (TCEQ)
Testimonials:
KDS Services is really great to deal with.-Consumer

We guarantee the services
of all pros displaying the
Done Right Guarantee® logo.

Map & Symbols

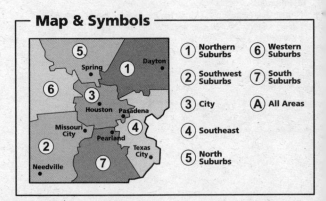

① Northern Suburbs
② Southwest Suburbs
③ City
④ Southeast
⑤ North Suburbs
⑥ Western Suburbs
⑦ South Suburbs
Ⓐ All Areas

PRESSURE WASHING CONT'D

MINUTEMAN BUILDING SERVICES, LLC
(888) 215-1336

(👍 Guaranteed)

Ⓐ

In Business Since: 1999
Best At: Brick, Building Exteriors, Concrete, Decks, Fencing, Patios, Roof Washing, Staining, Surfaces
Special Offers: 10% Done Right! Discount
Testimonials:

If you want an easy company to deal with you must use Minuteman Building Services. They are very nice.-Consumer

---

HOUSTON HOT WATER
(877) 390-3005

(👍 Guaranteed)

③

In Business Since: 1972
Best At: Brick, Building Exteriors, Concrete, Decks, Driveways, Fencing, Home Exteriors, Hydroblasting, Patios, Pool Decks, Power Washing, Residential & Commercial, Stain Removal, Wood Decks
Special Offers: Referral Discount
Testimonials:

I use him for pressure washing. I've used him many times, on many different properties. He's great. Not one problem.-Multi-unit Rental Property Owner/ Manager

REMODELING—BATHROOMS

FLOOR COVERINGS & MORE, INC.

(👍 Guaranteed)

Ⓐ

Address: 2395 Highway 6 South, Suite F
Houston, TX 77077

(877) 464-7037

In Business Since: 1989
Best At: Additions, Bathroom Fixtures & Accessories, Cabinet Refacing, Cabinets, Complete Remodels, Counter Tops, Custom Work, Flooring, Tile
Brands: KraftMaid
Special Offers: Two Year Financing with No Interest
Associations & Certifications: Texas Residential Construction Commission
Other Categories: Remodeling - Kitchens
Testimonials:

I highly recommend Floor Coverings & More. They are very friendly and easy to deal with.-Consumer

P

R

Every Call is Free!

Guaranteed Home Improvement Pros

- Free to Use

- Worry-Free and Guaranteed*

- Pre-Screened and Relentlessly Reviewed

- Contractors, Plumbers, Electricians and more

Also Online At
www.DoneRight.com

REMODELING—BATHROOMS CONT'D

LARR-WOOD CONSTRUCTION

👍 Guaranteed

①②③⑤⑥

Address: 19515 Wied Rd., Suite B
Spring, TX 77388

(877) 465-7795

In Business Since: 2001
Best At: Complete Remodels, Counter Tops, Cabinets, Repair, Restoration, Additions, Flooring, Sinks
Special Offers: Satisfaction Guarantee
Associations & Certifications: Texas Residential Construction Commission
Other Categories: Remodeling - Kitchens
Testimonials:

I've used Larr-Wood for over 6 years now. All I can say is that Larry has the most professional and reliable company. His crew does excellent work, and I have recommended Larr-Wood to everyone who needed his services.-General Contractor

REMODELING—KITCHENS

SEARS HOME IMPROVEMENT PRODUCTS

👍 Guaranteed

Ⓐ

(877) 329-6812

In Business Since: 1984
Best At: 100s of Drawer & Cabinet Styles & Colors, Cabinets, Counter Tops, Custom Cabinet Refacing, Hardware, Match any Styles, Sinks, Turnkey Installation
Brands: Aristokraft®, Corian®, DuPont™, Zodiaq®
Special Offers: Free Estimates
Associations & Certifications: Better Business Bureau, ENERGY STAR, Texas Residential Construction Commission

We guarantee the services
of all pros displaying the
Done Right Guarantee® logo.

REMODELING—KITCHENS CONT'D

FLOOR COVERINGS & MORE, INC.

Guaranteed (A)

Address: 2395 Highway 6 South, Suite F
Houston, TX 77077

(800) 840-1193

In Business Since: 1989
Best At: Additions, Cabinet Refacing, Cabinets, Carpentry, Complete Remodels, Counter Tops, Custom Cabinets, Flooring, Painting
Brands: Daltile®, Emser Tile®, KraftMaid, Mannington®, Pergo®, Quick-Step®
Special Offers: Two Year Financing with No Interest
Associations & Certifications: Texas Residential Construction Commission
Other Categories: Remodeling - Bathrooms
Testimonials:

I highly recommend Floor Coverings & More. They are very friendly and easy to deal with.-Consumer

LARR-WOOD CONSTRUCTION

Guaranteed ①②③⑤⑥

Address: 19515 Wied Rd., Suite B
Spring, TX 77388

(888) 893-9288

In Business Since: 2001
Best At: Additions, Cabinets, Complete Remodels, Counter Tops, Flooring, Repair, Restoration
Special Offers: Satisfaction Guarantee
Associations & Certifications: Texas Residential Construction Commission
Other Categories: Remodeling - Bathrooms
Testimonials:

I've used Larr-Wood for over 6 years now. All I can say is that Larry has the most professional and reliable company. His crew does excellent work, and I have recommended Larr-Wood to everyone who needed his services.-General Contractor

We guarantee the services
of all pros displaying the
Done Right Guarantee® logo.

REMODELING—NEW ADDITIONS

AMS REMODELING

  Guaranteed

 (3)

Address: 2107 Lou Ellen Ln.
Houston, TX 77018

(800) 953-5449

 BBB ACCREDITED BUSINESS bbb.org

In Business Since: 1988
Best At: All Home Remodeling, Bathroom Remodels, Complete Remodels, Custom Additions, Garages, Major Remodeling, New Homes, Room Additions
Associations & Certifications: Better Business Bureau, Texas Residential Construction Commission
Other Categories: Contractors - General Contractors
Testimonials:

I can't say enough about AMS Remodeling! I have used them personally and I have recommended their service to many of my clients.-Realtor

---

SAGE BUILT HOMES, LLC

  Guaranteed

(3)

Address: 2855 Mangum Rd., Suite 412
Houston, TX 77092

(888) 847-0943

In Business Since: 2005
Best At: Bathrooms, Complete Remodels, Consultation, Custom Additions, Design, Kitchens, Major Remodeling, New Homes
Associations & Certifications: Greater Houston Builders Association, Texas Residential Construction Commission
Testimonials:

Scott and his guys did a fantastic job building our new addition and remodeling our house. I highly recommend them to anyone looking to work with them. He's very detail-oriented and did a great job. We appreciated having him on board.-Consumer

ROOFING—CONTRACTORS

MURRAY ROOFING & CONSTRUCTION, LLC
(877) 416-4844

  Guaranteed

(A)

In Business Since: 1977
Best At: Asphalt Shingles, Cedar Shake Roofs, Certifications, Clay Tile, Coating, Sealing & Finishing, Composition Shingles, Concrete Tile, Flat Roofs, Replacement Roofs
Testimonials:

Murray Roofing was prompt, efficient, worked fast, cleaned up nicely, and kept us informed at all times. They did an overall great job.-Consumer

ROOFING—REPAIR

MURRAY ROOFING & CONSTRUCTION, LLC
(877) 414-1639

In Business Since: 1977
Best At: Asphalt Shingles, Certifications, Clay Tile, Coating, Sealing & Finishing, Composition Shingles, Concrete Tile, Emergency Service, Flat Roofs, Roof Repair, Shake Roof, Slate, Tile
Testimonials:
Murray Roofing was prompt, efficient, worked fast, cleaned up nicely and kept us informed at all times. They did an overall, great job.-Consumer

---

RM ROOFING
Address: 11600 Jones Rd., #108
Houston, TX 77070
(877) 206-2732

In Business Since: 1990
Best At: APP Modified Torchdown Flat Roofing, Asphalt Shingles, Composition Shingles, Emergency Service, Flat Roofs, Shingles, Tile Restoration, Waterproofing
Brands: Elk, TAMKO®
Associations & Certifications: Better Business Bureau, Houston Apartment Association
Testimonials:
We've used RM Roofing for 2 years now. They do a good job and I would recommend their service.-General Contractor

SCREENS

THE ENERGY SAVERS
(866) 708-7335

In Business Since: 1979
Best At: Stock & Custom Made Screens, Shades, Solar Sunscreens, Sunscreens, Storm Screens
Brands: Phifer SunTex®
Special Offers: Referral Program, Volume Discount
Testimonials:
They did a fine job and I would surely recommend them to all of my friends.-Consumer

Every Call is Free!

SECURITY SYSTEMS

PINNACLE SECURITY, LLC   👍 Guaranteed
(877) 427-1076   Ⓐ
In Business Since: 2001
License Number: B11753
Best At: Burglary, Fire, Home, Installation, 24-Hour Monitoring, Medical Emergency Assistance
Associations & Certifications: Better Business Bureau
Testimonials:

We were very impressed with the service provided by Pinnacle Security. They had an excellent training process. The system is easy to use and they had great communication with us through the entire process. We had a system installed at our business and are switching our current home system to Pinnacle. We recommend Pinnacle to all of our tenants.-Multi-unit Rental Property Owner/ Manager

SHUTTERS

CLASSIC WALLCOVERINGS, INC.   👍 Guaranteed
Address: 28155 State Hwy. 249, Suite 6B
Tomball, TX 77375   Ⓐ
(877) 584-5262
In Business Since: 1984
Best At: Cell Shades, Roller Shades, Arched & Angled Windows, Solar Shades, Woven Woods
Brands: Hunter Douglas, Royal™, Skandia, USA Shutters, Vista
Other Categories: Windows - Coverings & Treatments
Testimonials:

Classic Wallcoverings is a top notch company. They are very professional, dependable and keep me updated constantly. I highly recommend them.-Consumer

We guarantee the services
of all pros displaying the
Done Right Guarantee® logo.

SHUTTERS CONT'D

PRICED RIGHT BLINDS AND SHUTTERS

👍 Guaranteed
Ⓐ

Address: 17607 Lonesome Dove Trails
Houston, TX 77095

(888) 632-0038

In Business Since: 1957
Best At: Custom Made, Arched & Angled Windows, Poly Shutters, Hardwood Shutters, Motorized Shutters, Blinds, In-home Consultation, Design Preview
Other Categories: Blinds
Testimonials:

Priced Right Blinds and Shutters does great work and has excellent prices. I highly recommend his services.-Consumer

We guarantee the services
of all pros displaying the
Done Right Guarantee® logo.

Map & Symbols

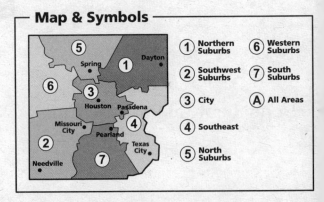

1 Northern Suburbs
2 Southwest Suburbs
3 City
4 Southeast
5 North Suburbs
6 Western Suburbs
7 South Suburbs
Ⓐ All Areas

SIDING

AMAZING SIDING CORPORATION

Address: 9825 FM 2920
Tomball, TX 77375

(888) 242-7398

In Business Since: 1989
Best At: Energy Efficiency, Gutters, Installation, Premium Siding, Vinyl, Vinyl Reinforced, Windows
Brands: Crane Performance Siding®, Renewal by Andersen®
Associations & Certifications: Better Business Bureau, National Association of the Remodeling Industry
Testimonials:

Amazing Siding did an incredible job on my home. Robert is a great guy to work with, and I have already recommended him to other friends.-Consumer

SEARS HOME IMPROVEMENT PRODUCTS
(877) 327-1618

In Business Since: 1984
Best At: Eaves, Energy Efficiency, Installation, Low Maintenance, Overhangs, Premium Vinyl Siding, Variety of Colors, Weather Resistant, Wood-grain Texture Panels
Brands: WeatherBeater
Special Offers: Free Estimates
Associations & Certifications: Better Business Bureau, ENERGY STAR

K & S RENOVATIONS
(888) 212-0991

In Business Since: 1995
Best At: Installation, Premium Siding, Vinyl & Fiber Cement Siding, Windows
Associations & Certifications: Better Business Bureau, Texas Residential Construction Commission
Testimonials:

K & S Renovations has done a complete renovation for me. I found them to be very reliable and they have proven to do great work. I will use them again when I have another remodeling project.-Consumer

S

Every Call is Free!

SOD & ARTIFICIAL TURF

MATA-TURF, INC.

Address: 10408 Tanner Rd.
Houston, TX 77041

(888) 290-7880

In Business Since: 1995
Best At: Delivery, Installation
Testimonials:

*Mata-Turf provided phenomenal, top class service. I highly recommend them.-
Consumer*

SPRINKLER SYSTEMS—REPAIR & MAINTENANCE

APS SPRINKLER SYSTEMS, INC.

Address: 11210 Rusty Pine Ln.
Tomball, TX 77375

(877) 322-5777

In Business Since: 1998
License Number: LI0009095
Best At: Automatic Valves, Drainage Systems, Drip Irrigation Systems, Emergency Service, Residential & Commercial, Timers, Valve Locating, Valves, Wiring, Sprinkler Re-Routing, Troubleshooting
Brands: Hunter®, Irritrol®, Rain Bird®, Toro®
Associations & Certifications: Better Business Bureau
Testimonials:

Caps Sprinkler Systems did an excellent job for me and they have great customer relations. I recommend their service to anyone.-Consumer

SUNRISE SPRINKLER SYSTEMS, INC.

(888) 528-2519

In Business Since: 1983
License Number: LI0005895
Best At: Automated Fertilizing Systems, Automated Pest Control Systems, Automatic Valves, Drainage Systems, Drip Irrigation Systems, Emergency Service, Filters, Piping, Pumps, PVC, Rain & Freeze Sensors, Residential & Commercial, Residential Repairs, Sprinkler Re-Routing, Surface Drains, Troubleshooting, Valve Locating, Valves, Wiring
Brands: Hunter®, Rain Bird®, Toro®
Special Offers: Free Estimates, Senior Citizen Discount
Associations & Certifications: Better Business Bureau, Houston Gulf Coast Irrigation Association (HGCIA)
Testimonials:

He put in full sprinkler systems, both front and back. He did a good job. I haven't had any problems. It's been about a year and they're still good. They work real well. I would recommend him. He's a stand up guy.-Consumer

SPRINKLER SYSTEMS—SALES & INSTALLATION

GREENSCAPE INNOVATIONS

Guaranteed

Address: P.O. BOX 3331
Conroe, TX 77305

(877) 427-4062

In Business Since: 2001
License Number: LI0008314
Best At: Drainage Systems, Leak Detection, Piping, Pumps, Residential & Commercial, Sprinklers, Timers
Brands: Hunter®, Rain Bird®
Associations & Certifications: Better Business Bureau
Testimonials:

He does all of my irrigation work. I'm a landscaper. We've been working together for about five or six years, and I've had no problems with him.-Member of the Trade

STUCCO

MINUTEMAN BUILDING SERVICES, LLC

Guaranteed

Ⓐ

(866) 540-4225

In Business Since: 1999
Best At: Cracks, Drywall, Exterior Coatings, Hydro Jetting, Painting, Patching, Re-stucco, Repair, Residential & Commercial, Sandblasting, Wall Damage
Special Offers: 10% Done Right! Discount
Other Categories: Decks, Floors - Coatings
Testimonials:

If you want an easy company to deal with you must use Minuteman Building Services. They are very nice.-Consumer

SUNROOMS

S

Every Call is Free!

TILE & STONE—CLEANING

SEARS CARPET, UPHOLSTERY & AIR DUCT CLEANING
(877) 416-4833

In Business Since: 1995
Best At: Deep Clean Ceramic Tile & Grout, Fully Enclosed Vacuum System, High Pressure Cleaning, Sealing, Tile & Stone Grout Cleaning
Special Offers: Discount for Done Right! Customers
Associations & Certifications: Better Business Bureau, Carpet & Rug Institute's Gold Seal of Approval
Other Categories: Carpet - Cleaning, Duct Cleaning, Emergency - Carpet Cleaning, Grout Cleaning, Upholstery - Cleaning & Restoration

ABSOLUTE KLEEN
(877) 356-6644

In Business Since: 1981
Best At: Cleaning, Deep Clean Ceramic Tile & Grout, Deep Cleaning, Grout, Grout & Tile Cleaning, High Pressure Cleaning, Natural Stone, Residential & Commercial
Special Offers: One Year Warranty
Associations & Certifications: Better Business Bureau

MARBLELIFE OF HOUSTON

Address: 7700 Renwick Dr., #4A
Houston, TX 77081
(888) 225-1558
In Business Since: 1991
Best At: Marble, Natural Stone, Natural Stone Polishing, Stone, Tile, Walls, Cleaning, Counter Tops, Floors, Grind Flat, Grout Dyeing, Interior & Exterior, Re-grouting, Repair, Restoration
Brands: MARBLELIFE® Stone Care Products
Associations & Certifications: Better Business Bureau
Testimonials:

Marblelife of Houston came in and cleaned and buffed our stone floors. They were great to work with and did an excellent job. I would definitely use them again and I have recommended their service to others.-Consumer

Every Call is Free!

TILE & STONE—SALES & INSTALLATION

BAY AREA PAINT & TILE
(888) 264-8226

In Business Since: 1985
Best At: Ceramic Tile, Granite, Installation, Marble, Natural Stone, Porcelain, Stone, Tile, Travertine, Staining
Special Offers: New Customer Discount
Associations & Certifications: Better Business Bureau
Other Categories: Painting - Interior

GOSEN GENERAL CONTRACTORS, INC.

Address: 10101 Southwest Freeway, Suite 315-320
Houston, TX 77074

(800) 983-0118

In Business Since: 1992
Best At: Backsplashes, Bathrooms, Ceramic Tile, Custom Design, Custom Floors, Decorative Tile, Granite, Grout, Hardwood Flooring, Kitchens, Porcelain, Refacing
Associations & Certifications: Better Business Bureau
Other Categories: Painting - Interior
Testimonials:

We've used Gosen General on several occasions, and we are always happy with their quality of work.-General Contractor

We guarantee the services
of all pros displaying the
Done Right Guarantee® logo.

TILE & STONE—SALES & INSTALLATION CONT'D

EMERALD TILE SERVICES

(👍 Guaranteed)
②③④⑥⑦

Address: P.O. Box 710842
Houston, TX 77271

(888) 853-9425

In Business Since: 1993
Best At: Ceramic Tile, Counter Tops, Floors, Kitchens, Bathrooms
Testimonials:
Emerald Tile Services does a great job! I will use their services again on my next project.-Consumer

PATTERSON CARPETS & INTERIORS, INC.

(👍 Guaranteed)
②③⑥

Address: 7026 Old Katy Rd., Suite 292
Houston, TX 77024

(877) 450-1527

In Business Since: 1991
Best At: Ceramic Tile, Counter Tops, Granite, Granite Slabs, Hardwood Flooring, Hardwood Refinishing, Hardwood Resurfacing, Marble, Natural Stone, Porcelain, Pre-finished Wood, Showers, Slate, Travertine
Other Categories: Floors - Sales & Installation
Testimonials:
They do a great job. They follow through to the completion with every project I have them do.-Consumer

We guarantee the services
of all pros displaying the
Done Right Guarantee® logo.

TREE CARE

TEXAS TREE TEAM
(800) 949-5887

In Business Since: 1997
Best At: Brush Chipping, Brush Trimming, Crown Reduction, Fire Prevention & Clean-up, Hedges, Insect & Disease Control, Irrigation, Pruning, Removal, Repair, Structural Trimming, Thinning, Tree & Shrub Planting, Tree & Stump Removal, Tree Trimming
Special Offers: Free Estimates
Associations & Certifications: Professional Landcare Network (PLANET)

OLVERA TREE SERVICES, INC.
(800) 934-6771

In Business Since: 1994
Best At: Brush Trimming, Pruning, Removal, Stump Removal, Thinning, Tree & Stump Removal, Tree Trimming
Special Offers: Free Estimates
Associations & Certifications: Better Business Bureau
Testimonials:

Olvera Tree Services has cut down several trees as well as done tree maintenance for me. They always work hard and do a good job. I will continue to use their service.-Consumer

---

FALL LANDSCAPE
Address: 16318 Alametos Dr.
Houston, TX 77083
(800) 934-3554

In Business Since: 1992
Best At: Brush Chipping, Brush Trimming, Hedges, Pruning, Removal, Tree & Shrub Planting, Tree & Stump Removal, Tree Trimming
Special Offers: Free Estimates
Testimonials:

We've worked with him for quite a while now. He's always done a great job for us. We love working with him. He's responsive, on time, does a good job, and we highly recommend him.-General Contractor

Every Call is Free!

UPHOLSTERY—CLEANING & RESTORATION

SEARS CARPET, UPHOLSTERY & AIR DUCT CLEANING
(877) 377-8871

Guaranteed
(A)

In Business Since: 1995
Best At: Heated Upholstery Cleaning Solutions, No Repairs, pH-Balancing Fiber Rinse, Two-step Deep-clean Process
Special Offers: Discount for Done Right! Customers
Associations & Certifications: Better Business Bureau, Carpet & Rug Institute's Gold Seal of Approval
Other Categories: Carpet - Cleaning, Duct Cleaning, Emergency - Carpet Cleaning, Grout Cleaning, Tile & Stone - Cleaning

OOPS STEAM CLEANING
(888) 565-8369

Guaranteed
(A)

In Business Since: 2006
Best At: Carpet Cleaning, Deep Steam Cleaning, Flood Damage, Pet Damage, Seat Covers, Stain Removal, Water Damage
Other Categories: Carpet - Cleaning

Every Call is Free!

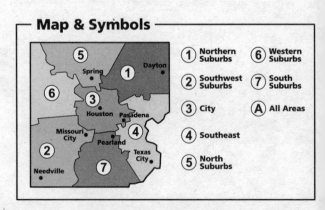

Map & Symbols

(1) Northern Suburbs
(2) Southwest Suburbs
(3) City
(4) Southeast
(5) North Suburbs
(6) Western Suburbs
(7) South Suburbs
(A) All Areas

WATER & FIRE DAMAGE—REPAIR & RESTORATION

ALLIED RECOVERY SERVICES
(888) 798-4680

👍 Guaranteed

Ⓐ

In Business Since: 1990
Best At: 24/7 Emergency Water Extraction, Carpet & Structural Drying, Complete Restoration, Damage Restoration, Dehumidification, Duct Cleaning, Emergency Service, Flood Damage, Moisture Detection, Mold Damage Restoration, Mold Remediation, Odor Control, Residential Experts, Vapor Barriers, Water Damage, Water Extraction

Associations & Certifications: Better Business Bureau, Indoor Air Quality Association (IAQA)
Other Categories: Mold - Removal & Abatement
Testimonials:

We've worked together for the last four years on an extensive amount of consulting on condo losses. We've also worked on $15 million worth of work for Church Mutual. Darryl is quite versatile and knowledgeable. I absolutely would recommend him.-Home Inspector

ADVANTAGE ENVIRONMENTAL SOLUTIONS
(800) 935-2556

👍 Guaranteed

Ⓐ

In Business Since: 2001
Best At: Carpet & Structural Drying, Dehumidification, Emergency Service, Flood Damage, Mold Damage Restoration, Mold Remediation, Water Damage, Water Extraction
Associations & Certifications: American Indoor Air Quality Council Certification, Institute of Inspection, Cleaning & Restoration Certification
Other Categories: Mold - Removal & Abatement
Testimonials:

Advantage Environmental always comes through. I trust them fully to do the work complete and to do it correctly the first time.-Consumer

We guarantee the services
of all pros displaying the
Done Right Guarantee® logo.

WATER & FIRE DAMAGE—WATER HEATERS

WATER & FIRE DAMAGE—REPAIR & RESTORATION CONT'D

APEX EMERGENCY SERVICES  Guaranteed
Address: 9227 Thomasville Dr.
Houston, TX 77064 Ⓐ

(888) 455-4889
In Business Since: 2003
Best At: 24/7 Emergency Water Extraction, Dehumidification, Sewage Spill Clean-up, Structural Drying
Associations & Certifications: Better Business Bureau
Testimonials:
Apex Emergency Services is a fine company. They do great work and I have no hesitation in recommending their services.-Consumer

LINDBERG SERVICES GROUP 👍 Guaranteed
Address: 66830 N. Eldridge Pkwy., Suite 301
Houston, TX 77041 Ⓐ

(888) 226-3819
In Business Since: 1987
Best At: 24/7 Emergency Water Extraction, Biohazard Removal, Dehumidification, Emergency Service, Fire Damage, Flood Damage, Mold Remediation, Odor Control, Remodeling
Associations & Certifications: Chamber of Commerce, Institute of Inspection, Cleaning & Restoration Certification
Testimonials:
Lindberg Services Group is very detail orientated, professional, and fantastic to deal with.-Consumer

WATER HEATERS

911 PLUMBING
(888) 843-4412 👍 Guaranteed
①②③⑤⑥
In Business Since: 1990
License Number: M-37412
Best At: Emergency Service, Gas Lines, Inspecting & Testing, Installation, Leak Repairs, New Installations, Piping, Preventative Maintenance, Re-piping, Repair, Service & Maintenance, Tankless Water Heaters
Special Offers: Discount for Done Right! Customers, Senior Citizen Discount
Testimonials:
We use 911 Plumbing on all of our store locations plumbing needs. They show up and do the job that needs to be done.-Multi-unit Rental Property Owner/ Manager

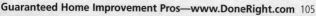

Guaranteed Home Improvement Pros—www.DoneRight.com 105

WINDOWS—CLEANING

FISH WINDOW CLEANING
(800) 889-0081

(👍 Guaranteed)

①②③⑤⑥

In Business Since: 1979
Best At: Chandeliers, Doors, Gutters, Interior & Exterior, Mirrors, Patio Glass, Skylights, Stain Removal
Special Offers: Free Estimates, Senior Citizen Discount

WINDOWS XPRESS
Address: 5526 Edith St.
  Houston, TX 77081
(800) 936-0119

(👍 Guaranteed)

③

In Business Since: 2005
Best At: 3-Step Cleaning Process, Chandeliers, Doors, Gutter Cleaning, Interior & Exterior, Maintenance, Patio Glass, Routine Scheduled Maintenance, Screens, Skylights, Stained Glass, Track Repair, Hand Washing, Window Waxing
Special Offers: Referral Discount
Testimonials:

We've used Windows Xpress on a few occasions. Their work is great and they are prompt. We will definitely use their service again.-Multi-unit Rental Property Owner/Manager

We guarantee the services
of all pros displaying the
Done Right Guarantee® logo.

WINDOWS—COVERINGS & TREATMENTS

CLASSIC WALLCOVERINGS, INC. 👍 Guaranteed

Ⓐ

Address: 28155 State Hwy. 249, Suite 6B
Tomball, TX 77375

(800) 934-2558

In Business Since: 1984
Best At: Cell Shades, Faux Blinds, Roller Shades, Romans, Shutters, Wood Blinds, Woven Woods, Arched & Angled Windows, Solar Shades
Brands: Hunter Douglas, Royal™, Skandia, USA Shutters, Vista
Associations & Certifications: Chamber of Commerce
Other Categories: Shutters
Testimonials:

> Classic Wallcoverings is a top notch company. They are very professional, dependable and keep me updated constantly. I highly recommend them.-Consumer

MAGNOLIA WINDOW COVERINGS 👍 Guaranteed

Ⓐ

Address: 35407-2 State Hwy. 249
Pinehurst, TX 77362

(877) 345-5230

In Business Since: 1989
Best At: Custom Window Coverings, Draperies, Faux Blinds, Full Service Supplier, Installation, Service, Shades, Shutters, Window Coverings, Wood Blinds
Brands: Fabricut, Hunter Douglas, Lafayette®, Skandia, Southland
Special Offers: Free In Home Constultation
Testimonials:

> Magnolia Window Coverings did a great job for us. We were very pleased with the consultation process and have referred them to several friends of ours.-Consumer

Every Call is Free!

WINDOWS—SALES & INSTALLATION

For repairs to window frames and hardware, please see our 'Handyman' section.

RENEWAL BY ANDERSEN

Address: 9825 FM 2920
Tomball, TX 77375

(888) 243-5614

In Business Since: 1989
Best At: Custom Windows, Design Center, Energy Efficiency, Exterior Restoration, Window Replacement, Stress Free
Brands: Andersen®, Fibrex®
Associations & Certifications: Better Business Bureau, ENERGY STAR, Greater Houston Builders Association, Green Seal Certification, National Association of the Remodeling Industry
Testimonials:

Renewal By Anderson did an incredible job on my home. Robert is a great guy to work with and I have already recommended him to other friends.-Consumer

---

SEARS HOME IMPROVEMENT PRODUCTS
(877) 334-8558

In Business Since: 1984
Best At: Custom-fit Windows, Energy Efficient & Low Maintenance, Grid Patterns, Interior Frame Color Option, Replacement, Vinyl Windows
Brands: WeatherBeater
Special Offers: Free Estimates
Associations & Certifications: Better Business Bureau, ENERGY STAR

Every Call is Free!

WINDOWS—TINTING

PRIVATE EYES SOLAR CONTROL (877) 444-3356

👍 Guaranteed

In Business Since: 2004
Best At: Anti-Graffiti, Custom Colors, Custom Tinting, Decorative Window Film, Heat Reduction, Home, Metallized Window Film, No Autos, Privacy Window Film, Residential & Commercial, Scratch Resistant, Security Window Film, UV Protection
Associations & Certifications: Better Business Bureau
Testimonials:

> The did an absolutely spectacular job. They were very quick to come out and work and the turnaround time was just one day. They were very professional and nice. I give them high marks for their work. I recommend them absolutely 100%.-Consumer

---

SUN TECH GLASS TINTING (888) 204-1913

👍 Guaranteed

In Business Since: 1983
Best At: Custom Tinting, Heat Reduction, No Autos, Privacy Window Film, Residential & Commercial
Testimonials:

> Sun Tech came in with professionalism and completed the job in no time at all.-Consumer

We guarantee the services
of all pros displaying the
Done Right Guarantee® logo.

Done Right! *Quick Pages*

Done Right's QuickPages are your quick reference for some of the top categories in home services and home improvement. All of the pros featured in Done Right's QuickPages are guaranteed.

CARPET—CLEANING

SEARS CARPET, UPHOLSTERY & AIR DUCT CLEANING
(888) 294-5786

OOPS STEAM CLEANING
(888) 563-5952

ABSOLUTE KLEEN
(888) 829-4809

CONTRACTORS—GENERAL CONTRACTORS

K & S RENOVATIONS
(888) 214-5715

DECKS

MINUTEMAN DECK AND FENCE STAINING
(877) 584-6259

K & S RENOVATIONS
(877) 416-3821

ELECTRICIANS

ARS/RESCUE ROOTER
(866) 269-8883

UNIVERSAL WIRING
(888) 843-4228

KENMOR ELECTRIC CO., LP
(888) 805-8390

LOGO ELECTRICAL SERVICES, INC.
(888) 841-1272

G & A ELECTRIC CO.
(800) 970-2798

FENCES

MINUTEMAN BUILDING SERVICES, LLC
(888) 847-0769

BRUSHSTROKES PAINTING, INC.
(888) 629-3635

FLOORS—REFINISHING & RESURFACING

FLOORS ETCETERA, INC.
(800) 920-2158

FLOORS—SALES & INSTALLATION

HOUSTON DESIGN CENTER
(888) 226-8559

WAYNE'S CARPET & OAK FLOORING
(888) 243-9340

GARAGE DOORS

PRECISION GARAGE DOOR SERVICE
(888) 216-6048

GUTTERS & DOWNSPOUTS—INSTALLATION & REPAIR

GUTTERMAXX, LP
(800) 927-2336

GUTTER PROFESSIONALS OF GREATER HOUSTON
(877) 378-8769

HANDYMAN

HANDYMAN CONNECTION
(877) 227-1558

RDZ CONSTRUCTION
(800) 964-7993

HEATING & COOLING—REPAIR & MAINTENANCE

ARS/RESCUE ROOTER
(888) 731-2921

SEARS HOME SERVICES
(877) 201-3317

LAWN CARE

TRUGREEN
(888) 595-0006

MAIDS & CLEANING SERVICES

MERRY MAIDS
(888) 798-4678

PAINTING—EXTERIOR

TURNKEY PAINTING, INC.
(888) 234-3105

BRUSHSTROKES PAINTING, INC.
(888) 839-0218

K & S RENOVATIONS
(888) 213-6612

PAINTING—INTERIOR

BRUSHSTROKES PAINTING, INC.
(888) 835-6784

K & S RENOVATIONS
(888) 214-4938

MCCAIN KITCHEN & BATH
(800) 934-1339

TURNKEY PAINTING, INC.
(888) 242-9307

Done Right! *Quick-Pages*

PEST CONTROL

TERMINIX
(888) 724-1220

HART PEST CONTROL & HORTICULTURAL SERVICES
(888) 273-4471

NATURE'S PEST SOLUTIONS
(888) 801-7137

PLUMBING—CONTRACTORS

ARS/RESCUE ROOTER
(888) 422-1794

SOUTHERN PLUMBING SERVICES, LLC
(877) 315-3914

ROOFING—CONTRACTORS

MURRAY ROOFING & CONSTRUCTION, LLC
(877) 416-4844

ROOFING—REPAIR

MURRAY ROOFING & CONSTRUCTION, LLC
(877) 414-1639

WINDOWS—SALES & INSTALLATION

RENEWAL BY ANDERSEN
(888) 243-5614

SEARS HOME IMPROVEMENT PRODUCTS
(877) 334-8558

NOTES

Guaranteed Home Improvement Pros

Quick Reference Card

Carpet—Cleaning

Sears Carpet, Upholstery &
Air Duct Cleaning
(888) 294-5786

Oops Steam Cleaning
(888) 563-5952

Contractors—

General Contractors

K & S Renovations
(888) 214-5715

Electricians

ARS/Rescue RoOter
(866) 269-8883

Universal Wiring
(888) 843-4228

Handyman

Handyman
Connection
(877) 227-1558

RDZ Construction
(800) 964-7993

Maids & Cleaning Services

Merry Maids
(888) 798-4678

Pest Control

Terminix
(888) 724-1220

Hart Pest Control &
Horticultural Services
(888) 273-4471

Plumbing—Contractors

ARS/Rescue Rooter
(888) 422-1794

Southern Plumbing
Services, LLC
(877) 315-3914

Roofing—Repair

Murray Roofing &
Construction, LLC
(877) 414-1639

Houston Directory

www.DoneRight.com

Index

Index

Index

Index